Berlitz®

Italia

phrase book & dictionary

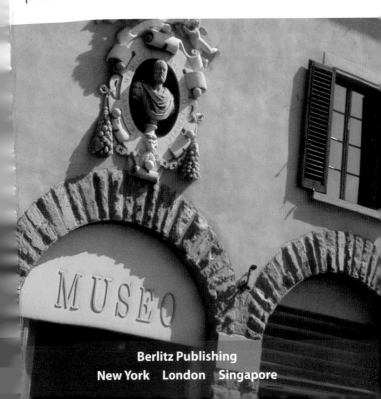

Berlitz Publishing
New York   London   Singapore

Contacting the Editors
Every effort has been made to provide accurate information in this publication, but changes are inevitable. The publisher cannot be responsible for any resulting loss, inconvenience or injury. We would appreciate it if readers would call our attention to any errors or outdated information. We also welcome your suggestions; if you come across a relevant expression not in our phrase book, please contact us at: **comments@berlitzpublishing.com**

All Rights Reserved
© 2018 Apa Digital (CH) AG and Apa Publications (UK) Ltd.
Berlitz Trademark Reg. U.S. Patent Office and other countries. Marca Registrada. Used under license from Berlitz Investment Corporation.

Thirteenth Printing: March 2018
Printed in China

Editor: Helen Fanthorpe
Translation: updated by Wordbank
Cover Design: Rebeka Davies
Interior Design: Beverley Speight

Picture Researcher: Tom Smyth
Cover Photos: All images iStock
Interior Photos: All photography Britta Jaschinski/APA except Kevin Cummins/APA 38; iStockphoto 131, 134, 138, 148, 149, 152; Lucy Johnston/APA 16, 174; Susan Smart/APA 107, 110, 126, 140, 144.

Distribution

UK, Ireland and Europe
Apa Publications (UK) Ltd
sales@insightguides.com
United States and Canada
Ingram Publisher Services
ips@ingramcontent.com
Australia and New Zealand
Woodslane
info@woodslane.com.au
Southeast Asia
Apa Publications (SN) Pte
singaporeoffice@insightguides.com

Worldwide
Apa Publications (UK) Ltd
sales@insightguides.com

Special Sales, Content Licensing, and CoPublishing
Discounts available for bulk quantities. We can create special editions, personalized jackets, and corporate imprints. sales@insightguides.com; www.insightguides.biz

Contents

Pronunciation	7	Vowels	8
Consonants	7	How to use this Book	10

Survival

Arrival & Departure	**13**	Parking	34
ESSENTIAL	13	Breakdown & Repair	34
Border Control	14	Accidents	35
Money	**15**	**Places to Stay**	**36**
ESSENTIAL	15	ESSENTIAL	36
At the Bank	16	Somewhere to Stay	37
		At the Hotel	37
Getting Around	**18**	Price	39
ESSENTIAL	18	Preferences	39
Tickets	19	Questions	40
Plane	21	Problems	41
Airport Transfer	21	Checking Out	42
Checking In	21	Renting	43
Luggage	23	Domestic Items	44
Finding your Way	24	At the Hostel	45
Train	24	Going Camping	46
Departures	26		
On Board	26	**Communications**	**47**
Bus	26	ESSENTIAL	47
Metro	28	Online	48
Boat & Ferry	29	Social Media	49
Taxi	30	Phone	51
Bicycle & Motorbike	31	Telephone Etiquette	53
Car Hire	31	Fax	54
Fuel Station	32	Post	55
Asking Directions	33		

Food & Drink

Eating Out 57
ESSENTIAL 57
Where to Eat 58
Reservations & Preferences 58
How to Order 60
Cooking Methods 62
Dietary Requirements 62
Dining with Children 63
How to Complain 63
Paying 64

Meals & Cooking 65
Breakfast 65
Appetizers 66
Soup 67
Fish & Seafood 68
Meat & Poultry 69

Vegetables & Staples 71
Fruit 73
Cheese 74
Dessert 75
Sauces & Condiments 77
At the Market 77
In the Kitchen 78

Drinks 80
ESSENTIAL 80
Non-alcoholic Drinks 81
Aperitifs, Cocktails & Liqueurs 82
Beer 83
Wine 84

On the Menu 85

People

Conversation 101
ESSENTIAL 101
Language Difficulties 101
Making Friends 103
Travel Talk 104
Personal 105
Work & School 106
Weather 107

Romance 108
ESSENTIAL 108
The Dating Game 108
Accepting & Rejecting 109
Getting Intimate 110
Sexual Preferences 110

Leisure Time

Sightseeing 112
ESSENTIAL 112
Tourist Information 112
On Tour 113
Seeing the Sights 114
Religious Sites 115

Shopping 116
ESSENTIAL 116
At the Shops 116
Ask an Assistant 118
Personal Preferences 119
Paying & Bargaining 120
Making a Complaint 122
Services 122
Hair & Beauty 123
Antiques 124
Clothing 124
Colors 125
Clothes & Accessories 125

Fabric 127
Shoes 127
Sizes 127
Newsagent & Tobacconist 128
Photography 128
Souvenirs 129

Sport & Leisure 131
ESSENTIAL 131
Watching Sport 132
Playing Sport 133
At the Beach/Pool 133
Winter Sports 135
Out in the Country 136

Going Out 137
ESSENTIAL 137
Entertainment 138
Nightlife 139

Special Requirements

Business Travel 141
ESSENTIAL 141
On Business 141

Traveling with Children 143
ESSENTIAL 143
Out & About 144

Baby Essentials 145
Babysitting 146
Health & Emergency 146

Disabled Travelers 147
ESSENTIAL 147
Asking for Assistance 148

In an Emergency

Emergencies 150
ESSENTIAL 150

Police 151
ESSENTIAL 151
Crime & Lost Property 151

Health 153
ESSENTIAL 153
Finding a Doctor 153
Symptoms 154
Conditions 155
Treatment 155
Hospital 156
Dentist 157
Gynecologist 157
Optician 157
Payment & Insurance 157
Pharmacy 158
ESSENTIAL 158
What to Take 159

Basic Supplies 160

The Basics 162
Grammar 162
Numbers 167
ESSENTIAL 167
Ordinal Numbers 168
Time 169
ESSENTIAL 169
Days 169
ESSENTIAL 169
Dates 170
Months 170
Seasons 171
Holidays 171
Conversion Tables 172
Kilometers to Miles Conversions 172
Measurement 172
Temperature 173
Oven Temperature 173

Dictionary

English-Italian Dictionary 175
Italian-English Dictionary 200

Pronunciation

This section is designed to make you familiar with the sounds of Italian using our simplified phonetic transcription. You'll find the pronunciation of the Italian letters and sounds explained below, together with their 'imitated' equivalents. This system is used throughout the phrase book; simply read the pronunciation as if it were English, noting any special rules below.

Stress has been indicated in the phonetic pronunciations by underlining. These letters should be pronounced with more emphasis. Generally, the vowel of the next to last syllable is stressed. When a final vowel is stressed, it has an accent.

Consonants

Letter(s)	Approximate Pronunciation	Symbol	Example	Pronunciation
c	1. before e and i, ch as in chip	ch	cerco	_chehr_·koh
	2. elsewhere, c as in cat	k	conto	_kohn_·toh
ch	c as in cat	k	che	keh
g	1. before e and i, like j in jet	j	valigia	vah·_lee_·jyah
	2. elsewhere, g as in go	g	grande	_grahn_·deh
gg	pronounced more intensely	dj	viaggio	_vyah_·djoh
gh	g as in go	gh	ghiaccio	_ghyah_·chyoh
gli	lli as in million	lly	bagaglio	bah·_gah_·llyoh
gn	like the first n in onion	ny	bagno	_bah_·nyoh
h	always silent		ha	ah

Letter(s)	Approximate Pronunciation	Symbol	Example	Pronunciation
r	rolled in the back of the mouth	r	**Roma**	_roh_•mah
s	1. generally s as in sit	s	**salsa**	_sahl_•sah
	2. sometimes z as in zoo	z	**casa**	_kah_•zah
sc	1. before e and i, sh as in shut	sh	**uscita**	oo•_shee_•tah
	2. elsewhere, sk as in skin	sk	**scarpa**	_skahr_•pah
z/zz	1. generally ts as in hits	ts	**grazie**	_grah_•tsyeh
	2. sometimes a little softer, like dz	dz	**zero**	_dzeh_•roh

The letters b, d, f, k, l, m, n, p, q, t and v are pronounced as in English. The letters j, k, w, x and y are not true members of the Italian alphabet and appear only in foreign words or names.

Vowels

Letter	Approximate Pronunciation	Symbol	Example	Pronunciation
a	short, as in father	ah	**gatto**	_gaht_•toh
e	1. like e as in get	eh	**destra**	_deh_•strah
	2. before a single consonant, sometimes like e in they	ay	**sete**	_say_•teh

Letter	Approximate Pronunciation	Symbol	Example	Pronunciation
i	ee as in meet	**ee**	**vini**	_vee_•nee
o	o as in so	**oh**	**sole**	_soh_•leh
u	oo as in boot	**oo**	**fumo**	_foo_•moh

Vowel Combinations

Letter	Symbol	Example	Pronunciation
ae	**ah•eh**	**paese**	pah•_eh_•zeh
ao	**ah•oh**	**Paolo**	_pah_•oh•loh
au	**ow**	**auto**	_ow_•toh
eo	**eh•oh**	**museo**	moo•_zeh_•oh
eu	**eh•oo**	**euro**	_eh_•oo•roh
ei	**ay**	**lei**	lay
ia	**yah**	**piazza**	_pyah_•tsah
ie	**yeh**	**piede**	_pyeh_•deh
io	**yoh**	**piove**	_pyoh_•veh
iu	**yoo**	**più**	pyoo
ua	**wah**	**quale**	_kwah_•leh
ue	**weh**	**questo**	_kweh_•stoh
ui	**wee**	**qui**	kwee
uo	**woh**	**può**	pwoh

There are approximately 60 million Italian speakers. Many different dialects add variety and color to the country's linguistic landscape. In addition, Italian is spoken in the southern area of Switzerland.

How to use this Book

Sometimes you see two alternatives separated by a slash. Choose the one that's right for your situation.

ESSENTIAL

I'm on vacation [holiday]/business.

Sono in vacanza/viaggio d'affari.
soh•noh een vah•kahn•tsah/vyah•djoh dahf•fah•ree

I'm going to...

Vado a ... *vah•doh ah ...*

I'm staying at the...Hotel.

Sono all'hotel ... *soh•noh ahl•loh•tehl ...*

Words you may see are shown in YOU MAY SEE boxes.

YOU MAY SEE...

DOGANA	customs
MERCE DUTY-FREE	duty-free goods
MERCE DA DICHIARARE	goods to declare

Any of the words or phrases listed can be plugged into the sentence below.

Tickets

When's the...to Milan?

A che ora è il/l...per Milano? *ah keh oh•rah eh eel/l...pehr mee•lah•noh*

(first) bus

(primo) autobus *(pree•moh) ow•toh•boos*

(next) flight

(prossimo) volo *(prohs•see•moh) voh•loh*

(last) train

(ultimo) treno *(ool•tee•moh) treh•noh*

Italian phrases appear in purple.

Read the simplified pronunciation as if it were English. For more on pronunciation, see page 7.

Personal

Who are you with? **Con chi è?** *kohn kee ee*
I'm here alone. **Sono da solo** *m* **/sola** *f.*
soh•noh dah soh•loh /soh•lah

When's your **Quando è il suo compleanno?**
birthday? *kwahn•doh eh eel soo•oh kohm•pleh•ahn•noh*
For Grammar, see page 162.

Related phrases can be found by going to the page number indicated.

When different gender forms apply, the masculine form is followed by *m*; feminine by *f*

A handshake is a common gesture among strangers or in formal settings. Traditionally, it is expected that a woman be the first to offer her hand. A kiss on both cheeks is used among friends and relatives. A nod and a smile suffice when greeting members of a group of people.

Information boxes contain relevant country, culture and language tips.

Expressions you may hear are shown in You May Hear boxes.

YOU MAY HEAR...

Parlo poco inglese. *pahr•loh poh•koh*
een•gleh•zeh
Non parlo inglese. *nohn pahr•loh een•gleh•zeh*

I only speak a little English.
I don't speak English.

Color-coded side bars identify each section of the book.

Survival

Arrival & Departure   13
Money   15
Getting Around   18
Places to Stay   36
Communications   47

Arrival & Departure

ESSENTIAL

I'm on vacation [holiday]/business.	**Sono in vacanza/viaggio d'affari.** _soh_•noh een vah•_kahn_•tsah/_vyah_•djoh dahf•_fah_•ree
I'm going to...	**Vado a...** _vah_•doh ah...
I'm staying at the...Hotel.	**Sono all'hotel...** _soh_•noh ahl•loh•_tehl_...

YOU MAY HEAR...

Il passaporto, per favore. eel pahs•sah•_pohr_•toh pehr fah•_voh_•reh	Your passport, please.
Motivo della visita? moh•_tee_•voh _dehl_•lah _vee_•zee•tah	What's the purpose of your visit?
Dove alloggia? _doh_•veh ahl•_loh_•djah	Where are you staying?
Quanto tempo si ferma? _kwahn_•toh _tehm_•poh see _fehr_•mah	How long are you staying?
Chi viaggia con Lei? kee _vyah_•djah kohn lay	Who are you traveling with?

Per favore is the standard Italian translation for 'please.'
Prego is the standard Italian translation for 'you are welcome,'
but it's also used for 'please,' in the sense of 'if you please,' in certain
informal situations.

Border Control

I'm just passing through.	**Sono solo di passaggio.** _soh•noh soh•loh dee pahs•sah•djoh_
I'd like to declare…	**Vorrei dichiarare…** _vohr•ray dee•kyah•rah•reh…_
I have nothing to declare.	**Non ho nulla da dichiarare.** _nohn oh nool•lah dah dee•kyah•rah•reh_

YOU MAY HEAR…

Ha qualcosa da dichiarare?
ah kwahl•koh•zah dah dee•kyah•rah•reh

Anything to declare?

Deve pagare la tassa su questo. _deh•veh pah•gah•reh lah tahs•sah soo kweh•stoh_

You must pay duty on this.

Apra questa borsa. _ah•prah kweh•stah bohr•sah_

Open this bag.

YOU MAY SEE…

DOGANA	customs
MERCE DUTY-FREE	duty-free goods
MERCE DA DICHIARARE	goods to declare
NULLA DA DICHIARARE	nothing to declare
CONTROLLO PASSAPORTI	passport control
POLIZIA	police

Money

ESSENTIAL

Where's...?	**Dov'è...?** *doh•veh*...
the ATM	**il bancomat** *eel bahn•koh•maht*
the bank	**la banca** *lah bahn•kah*
the currency exchange office	**l'ufficio di cambio** *loof•fee•chyoh dee kahm•byoh*
When does the bank open/close?	**A che ora apre/chiude la banca?** *ah keh oh•rah ah•preh/kyoo•deh lah bahn•kah*
I'd like to change dollars/pounds into euros.	**Vorrei cambiare dei dollari/delle sterline in euro.** *vohr•ray kahm•byah•reh day dohl•lah•ree/dehl•leh stehr•lee•neh een eh•oo•roh*
I'd like to cash traveler's checks [cheques].	**Vorrei riscuotere dei travellers cheques.** *vohr•ray ree•skwoh•teh•reh day trah•vehl•lehrs chehks*

At the Bank

I'd like to change money. **Vorrei cambiare del denaro.**
vohr•ray kahm•byah•reh dehl deh•nah•roh

How much is the fee? **Quant'è la commissione?** *kwahn•teh lah kohm•mees•syoh•neh*

I lost my traveler's checks [cheques]/ credit card. **Ho perso i miei travellers cheques/ la mia carta di credito.** *oh pehr•soh ee mee•ay trah•vehl•lehrs chehks/lah mee•ah kahr•tah dee kreh•dee•toh*

My card was stolen/doesn't work. **La mia carta di credito è stata rubata/non funziona.** *lah mee•ah kahr•tah dee kreh•dee•toh eh stah•tah roo•bah•tah/nohn foon•tsyoh•nah*

YOU MAY SEE...

Italian currency is the **euro €**, divided into 100 **centesimi**.
Coins: 1, 2, 5, 10, 20, 50 **cent.**; €1, 2
Notes: €5, 10, 20, 50, 100, 200, 500

YOU MAY SEE...

INSERIRE LA CARTA	insert card here
ANNULLA	cancel
CANCELLA	clear
CONFERMA	enter
CODICE SEGRETO	PIN
PRELIEVO	withdrawal
DEPOSITO	deposit
DA CONTO CORRENTE	from checking [current] account
DA CONTO DI RISPARMIO	from savings account
RICEVUTA	receipt

Cash can be obtained from ATMs with Visa™, Eurocard™, American Express® and many other international cards. Instructions are usually available in English. You can change money at travel agencies and hotels, but the rate will not be as good as at a bank or currency exchange office. Remember to bring your passport when you want to change money.

Getting Around

ESSENTIAL

How do I get to town?	**Come si arriva in città?** _koh•meh see ahr•ree•vah een cheet•tah_
Where's...?	**Dov'è...?** _doh•veh..._
the airport	**l'aeroporto** _lah•eh•roh•pohr•toh_
the train [railway] station	**la stazione ferroviaria** _lah stah•tsyoh•neh fehr•roh•vyah•ryah_
the bus station	**la stazione degli autobus** _lah stah•tsyoh•neh deh•llyee ow•toh•boos_
the metro [underground] station	**la stazione della metropolitana** _lah stah•tsyoh•neh dehl•lah meh•troh•poh•lee•tah•nah_
How far is it?	**Quanto dista?** _kwahn•toh dees•tah_
Where do I buy a ticket?	**Dove si comprano i biglietti?** _doh•veh see kohm•prah•noh ee bee•llyeht•tee_
A one-way/ return-trip ticket to...	**Un biglietto di andata/di andata e ritorno per...** _oon bee•llyeht•toh dee ahn•dah•tah/ dee ahn•dah•tah eh ree•tohr•noh pehr..._
How much?	**Quant'è?** _kwahn•teh_
Is there a discount?	**C'è uno sconto?** _cheh oon•oh skohn•toh_
Which...?	**Quale...?** _kwah•leh..._
gate	**uscita** _oo•shee•tah_
line	**linea** _lee•neh•ah_
platform	**binario** _bee•nah•ryoh_
Where can I get a taxi?	**Dove posso trovare un taxi?** _doh•veh pohs•soh troh•vah•reh oon tah•ksee_

Take me to this address.	**Mi porti a questo indirizzo.** *mee pohr•tee*
	ah kweh•stoh een•dee•ree•tsoh
Where's the car rental [hire]?	**Dov'è un autonoleggio?** *doh•veh oon*
	ow•toh•noh•leh•djoh
Can I have a map?	**Può darmi una cartina?** *pwoh dahr•mee oo•nah*
	kahr•tee•nah

Tickets

When's the...to Milan?	**A che ora è il/l'...per Milano?** *ah keh oh•rah*
	eh eel/l...pehr mee•lah•noh
(first) bus	**(primo) autobus** *(pree•moh) ow•toh•boos*
(next) flight	**(prossimo) volo** *(prohs•see•moh) voh•loh*
(last) train	**(ultimo) treno** *(ool•tee•moh) treh•noh*
Where do I buy a ticket?	**Dove si comprano i biglietti?** *doh•veh see*
	kohm•prah•noh ee bee•llyeht•tee
One/Two ticket(s), please.	**Un biglietto/Due biglietti, per favore.** *oon*
	bee•llyeht•toh/doo•eh bee•llyeht•tee pehr fah•voh•reh
For today/tomorrow.	**Per oggi/domani.** *pehr oh•djee/doh•mah•nee*
A...ticket.	**Un biglietto...** *oon bee•llyeht•toh...*
one-way	**di andata** *dee ahn•dah•tah*
return-trip	**di andata e ritorno** *dee ahn•dah•tah eh ree•tohr•noh*
first class	**di prima classe** *dee pree•mah klahs•seh*
business class	**Biglietti di business class** *bee•llyeht•tee dee*
	beez•nehs klahs
second class	**di seconda classe** *dee seh•kohn•dah klahs•seh*
economy class	**di classe economica**
	dee klahs•seh eh•koh•noh•mee•kah
How much?	**Quant'è?** *kwahn•teh*

Is there a... discount?	**C'è un biglietto ridotto per...?** *cheh oon bee-llyeht-toh ree-doht-toh pehr...*
child	**bambini** *bahm-bee-nee*
student	**studenti** *stoo-dehn-tee*
senior citizen	**anziani** *ahn-tsyah-nee*
tourist	**turisti** *too-ree-stee*

The express/local bus/train, please. **L'autobus/Il treno espresso/locale, per favore.** *low-toh-boos/eel treh-noh eh-sprehs-soh/ loh-kah-leh pehr fah-voh-reh*

I have an e-ticket. **Ho un biglietto elettronico.** *oh oon bee-llyeht-toh eh-leht-troh-nee-koh*

Can I buy a ticket on the bus/train? **Posso comprare il biglietto sull'autobus/ sul treno?** *pohs-soh kohm-prah-reh eel bee-llyeht-toh sool-low-toh-boos/sool treh-noh*

Do I have to stamp the ticket before boarding? **Devo obliterare/timbrare il biglietto prima di salire a bordo?** *deh-voh oh-blee-teh-rah-reh/teem-brah-reh eel bee-llyeht-toh pree-mah dee sah-lee-reh ah bohr-doh?*

How long is this ticket valid? **Per quanto tempo è valido questo biglietto?** *pehr kwahn-toh tehm-poh eh vah-lee-doh kweh-stoh bee-llyeht-toh*

Can I return on the same ticket? **Posso fare il viaggio di ritorno con lo stesso biglietto?** *pohs-soh fah-reh eel vyah-djoh dee ree-tohr-noh kohn loh stehs-soh bee-llyeht-toh*

I'd like to...my reservation.	**Vorrei...la prenotazione.** *vohr-ray...lah preh-noh-tah-tsyoh-neh*
cancel	**annullare** *ahn-nool-lah-reh*
change	**cambiare** *kahm-byah-reh*
confirm	**confermare** *kohn-fehr-mah-reh*

For Days, see page 169.
For Time, see page 169.

Plane

Airport Transfer

How much is a taxi to the airport?	**Quant'è la tariffa del taxi fino all'aeroporto?** *kwahn•teh lah tah•reef•fah dehl tah•ksee fee•noh ahl•lah•eh•roh•pohr•toh*
To...Airport, please.	**All'aeroporto di..., per favore.** *ahl•lah•eh•roh•pohr•toh dee...pehr fah•voh•reh*
My airline is...	**Parto con la/l'...** *pahr•toh kohn lah/l...*
My flight leaves at...	**Il volo è alle...** *eel voh•loh eh ahl•leh...*
I'm in a rush.	**Ho fretta.** *oh freht•tah*
Can you take an alternate route?	**Può prendere un'altra strada?** *pwoh prehn•deh•reh oo•nahl•trah strah•dah*
Can you drive faster/slower?	**Può andare più velocemente/lentamente?** *pwoh ahn•dah•reh pyoo veh•loh•cheh•mehn•teh/ lehn•tah•mehn•teh*

YOU MAY HEAR...

Con che compagnia aerea viaggia? *kohn keh kohm•pah•nee•ah ah•eh•reh•ah vyah•djah*	What airline are you flying?
Nazionale o internazionale? *nah•tsyoh•nah•leh oh een•tehr•nah•tsyoh•nah•leh*	Domestic or international?
Quale terminal? *kwah•leh tehr•mee•nahl*	What terminal?

Checking In

Where's check-in?	**Dov'è il check-in?** *doh•veh eel chehk•een*
My name is...	**Mi chiamo...** *mee kyah•moh...*
I'm going to...	**Vado a...** *vah•doh ah...*

YOU MAY SEE...

ARRIVI	arrivals
PARTENZE	departures
RITIRO BAGAGLI	baggage claim
SICUREZZA	security
VOLI NAZIONALI	domestic flights
VOLI INTERNAZIONALI	international flights
CHECK-IN	check-in
CHECK-IN CON BIGLIETTO ELETTRONICO	e-ticket check-in
USCITA	exit

I have...	**Ho** *oh*
one suitcase	**una valigia** *oo•nah vah•lee•jyah*
two suitcases	**due valigie** *doo•eh vah•lee•jyeh*
one piece of hand luggage	**un bagaglio a mano** *oon bah•gah•llyoh ah mah•noh*
How much luggage is allowed?	**Quanti bagagli si possono portare?** *kwahn•tee bah•gah•llyee see pohs•soh•noh pohr•tah•reh*
Is that pounds or kilos?	**È in libbre o in chili?** *eh een leeb•breh oh een kee•lee*
Which terminal/ gate?	**Quale terminal/uscita?** *kwah•leh tehr•mee•nahl/ oo•shee•tah*
I'd like a window/ an aisle seat.	**Vorrei un posto vicino al finestrino/al corridoio.** *vohr•ray oon poh•stoh vee•chee•noh ahl fee•neh•stree•noh/ahl kohr•ree•doh•yoh*
When do we leave/arrive?	**Quando partiamo/arriviamo?** *kwahn•doh pahr•tyah•moh/ahr•ree•vyah•moh*
Is the flight delayed?	**Il volo è in ritardo?** *eel voh•loh eh een ree•tahr•doh*
How late?	**Di quanto è in ritardo?** *dee kwahn•toh eh een ree•tahr•doh*

Luggage

Where is/Where are...?	**Dov'è/Dove sono...?** doh•_veh_/doh•veh _soh_•noh...
the luggage carts [trolleys]	**i carrelli per i bagagli** ee kahr•_rehl_•lee pehr ee bah•_gah_•llyee
the luggage lockers	**il deposito bagagli** eel deh•_poh_•see•toh bah•_gah_•lyee

YOU MAY HEAR...

Il prossimo! eel _prohs_•see•moh	Next!
Il suo passaporto/biglietto, per favore. eel _soo_•oh pahs•sah•_pohr_•toh/bee•_llyeht_•toh pehr fah•_voh_•reh	Your passport/ticket, please.
Quanti bagagli consegna? _kwahn_•tee bah•_gah_•llyee kohn•_seh_•nyah	How many bags are you checking?
Ha il bagaglio in eccesso. ah eel bah•_gah_•llyoh een eh•_chehs_•soh	You have excess luggage.
È troppo grande per portarlo a mano. eh _trohp_•poh _grahn_•deh pehr pohr•_tahr_•loh ah _mah_•noh	That's too large for a carry-on [piece of hand luggage].
Ha fatto Lei le valigie? ah _faht_•toh lay leh vah•_lee_•jyeh	Did you pack these bags yourself?
Qualcuno le ha dato qualcosa da portare? kwahl•_koo_•noh leh ah _dah_•toh kwahl•_koh_•zah dah pohr•_tah_•reh	Did anyone give you anything to carry?
Vuoti le tasche. _vwoh_•tee leh _tahs_•keh	Empty your pockets.
Tolga le scarpe. _tohl_•gah leh _skahr_•peh	Take off your shoes.
Imbarco immediato... eem•_bahr_•koh eem•meh•_dyah_•toh...	Now boarding...

the baggage claim	**il ritiro bagagli** *eel ree·tee·roh bah·gah·llyee*
My luggage has been lost/stolen.	**Mi hanno perso/rubato i bagagli.** *mee ahn·noh pehr·soh/roo·bah·toh ee bah·gah·llyee*
My suitcase has been damaged.	**La mia valigia è danneggiata.** *lah mee·ah vah·lee·jyah eh dahn·neh·djah·tah*

Finding your Way

Where is/Where are…?	**Dov'è/Dove sono…?** *doh·veh/doh·veh soh·noh…*
the currency exchange	**il cambio valuta** *eel kahm·byoh vah·loo·tah*
the car rental [hire]	**l'autonoleggio** *l·ow·toh·noh·leh·djoh*
the exit	**l'uscita** *loo·shee·tah*
the taxis	**i taxi** *ee tah·ksee*
Is there… into town?	**C'è…per andare in città?** *cheh…pehr ahn·dah·reh een cheet·tah*
a bus	**un autobus** *oon ow·toh·boos*
a train	**un treno** *oon treh·noh*
a subway [underground]	**una metropolitana** *oo·nah meh·troh·poh·lee·tah·nah*

For Asking Directions, see page 33.

Train

Where's the train [railway] station?	**Dov'è la stazione ferroviaria?** *doh·veh lah stah·tsyoh·neh fehr·roh·vyah·ryah*
How far is it?	**Quanto dista?** *kwahn·toh dees·tah*
Where is/ Where are…?	**Dov'è/Dove sono…?** *doh·veh/doh·veh soh·noh…*
the ticket office	**la biglietteria** *lah bee·llyeht·teh·ree·ah*
the information	**l'ufficio informazioni** *loof·fee·chyoh*

YOU MAY SEE...

BINARI	platforms
INFORMAZIONI	information
PRENOTAZIONI	reservations
SALA D'ATTESA	waiting room
ARRIVI	arrivals
PARTENZE	departures

desk		een•fohr•mah•tsyoh•nee
the luggage	**il deposito bagagli**	eel deh•poh•see•toh
lockers		bah•gah•llyee
the platforms	**i binari**	ee bee•nah•ree
Can I have a	**Mi può dare un orario?**	mee pwoh dah•reh
schedule [timetable]?		oon oh•rah•ryoh
How long is	**Quanto dura il viaggio?**	kwahn•toh doo•rah
the trip?		eel vyah•djoh
Do I have to	**Devo cambiare?**	deh•voh kahm•byah•reh
change trains?		

For Asking Directions, see page 33.

For Tickets, see page 19.

Rail travel is extremely popular and one of the best ways to see Italy, especially with the faster—and more expensive—trains that link major cities. **Eurostar** and **InterCity** are the fastest trains, while **diretti**, **regionali** and **interregionali** are local trains—ideal to reach smaller towns. Tickets must be stamped before travel in one of the many machines on station concourses and platforms.

Italians use the 24-hour clock in schedules and other official
documents and situations. In other words, the morning hours from
1:00 a.m. to 12:00 noon are the same as in English; after that, just add
12. So, 1:00 p.m. would be 13:00, 5:00 p.m. would be 17:00 and so on.

Departures

Which track [platform] to...?	**Da che binario parte il treno per...?** *dah keh bee·nah·ryoh pahr·teh eel treh·noh pehr...*
Is this the track [platform]/train to...?	**È il binario/treno per...?** *eh eel bee·nah·ryoh/treh·noh pehr...*
Where is track [platform]...?	**Dov'è il binario...?** *doh·veh eel bee·nah·ryoh...*
Where do I change for...?	**Dove devo cambiare per...?** *doh·veh deh·voh kahm·byah·reh pehr...*

On Board

Can I sit here/open the window?	**Posso sedermi qui/aprire il finestrino?** *pohs·soh seh·dehr·mee kwee/ah·pree·reh eel fee·neh·stree·noh*
That's my seat.	**Questo posto è mio.** *kweh·stoh poh·stoh eh mee·oh*
Here's my reservation.	**Ecco la mia prenotazione** *ek·koh lah mee·ah preh·noh·tah·tsyoh·neh*

Bus

Where's the bus station?	**Dov'è la stazione degli autobus?** *doh·veh lah stah·tsyoh·neh deh·llyee ow·toh·boos*
How far is it?	**Quanto dista?** *kwahn·toh dees·tah*
How do I get to...?	**Come si arriva a...?** *koh·meh see ahr·ree·vah ah...*
Is this the bus to...?	**È l'autobus per...?** *eh low·toh·boos pehr...*
Can you tell me when to get off?	**Può dirmi quando scendere?** *pwoh deer·mee kwahn·doh shehn·deh·reh*

YOU MAY HEAR...

Biglietti, per favore. bee·_llyeht_·tee pehr
fah·_voh_·reh

Deve cambiare a Parma. _deh_·veh
kahm·_byah_·reh ah _pahr_·mah

Prossima fermata: Pisa. _prohs_·see·mah
fehr·_mah_·tah _pee_·zah

Tickets, please.

You have to change
at Parma.
Next stop, Pisa.

Do I have to change buses?	**Devo cambiare (autobus)?** _deh_·voh kahm·_byah_·reh (_ow_·toh·boos)
Stop here, please!	**Si fermi qui, per favore!** see _fehr_·mee kwee pehr fah·_voh_·reh

For Tickets, see page 19.

YOU MAY SEE...

FERMATA AUTOBUS	bus stop
ENTRATA/USCITA	enter/exit
CONVALIDA BIGLIETTO	stamp your ticket

When traveling by bus, purchase your ticket before boarding
from a tobacconist or from a vending machine at train or subway
stations. Tickets have a magnetic strip on the back. Upon boarding the
bus, validate your ticket at one of the yellow validation machines on the
bus (see picture on page 28). Insert your ticket into the machine with the
arrow toward you and pointing downward. The machine will accept the
ticket and then return it; a green light shows the ticket is valid and a red
light means it is invalid. If the machine does not work, you can try another
machine on the bus or write the date, time of day and the bus number
on the ticket. If the bus features only the older orange machines, fold the
ticket in half lengthwise so that it fits into the machine for validation.

Metro

Where's the metro [underground] station?	**Dov'è la stazione della metropolitana?** doh·_veh_ lah stah·_tsyoh_·neh _dehl_·lah meh·troh·poh·lee·_tah_·nah
A map, please.	**Una cartina, per favore.** _oo_·nah kahr·_tee_·nah pehr fah·_voh_·reh
Which line for…?	**Che linea devo prendere per…?** keh _lee_·neh·ah _deh_·voh _prehn_·deh·reh pehr…
Which direction?	**In quale direzione?** een kwah·leh dee·reh·_tsyoh_·neh

The Italian public transportation system is extensive and
generally efficient. Urban areas are served by networks of buses,
trams and subways. Tickets are usually sold at **edicole** (newsstands),
nearby **caffè** (coffee bars) and **tabacchi** (tobacconists). Discounts are
available but vary between locations. Ask the hotel concierge or your
travel agent for a schedule.

Do I have to transfer [change]?	**Devo cambiare?** _deh_•voh kahm•_byah_•reh
Is this the subway [train] to…?	**È la metropolitana per…?** _eh lah meh•troh•poh•lee•_tah_•nah pehr…_
How many stops to…?	**Quante fermate mancano per arrivare a…?** _kwahn•teh fehr•mah•teh mahn•kah•noh pehr ahr•ree•vah•reh ah_
Where are we?	**Dove siamo?** _doh_•veh _syah_•moh

For Tickets, see page 19.

YOU MAY SEE…

| IMBARCAZIONE DI SALVATAGGIO | life boat |
| GIUBBOTTO DI SALVATAGGIO | life jacket |

Boat & Ferry

When is the ferry to…?	**Quando parte il traghetto per…?** _kwahn_•doh _pahr_•teh eel trah•_gheht_•toh pehr…
Can I take my car?	**Posso portare l'auto?** _pohs_•soh pohr•_tah_•reh l•_ow_•toh
What time is the next sailing?	**A che ora è la prossima partenza?** _ah keh oh•rah eh lah prohs•see•mah pahr•tehn•tsah_
Can I book a seat/cabin?	**Posso prenotare un posto/una cabina?** _pohs_•soh preh•noh•_tah_•reh oon poh•stoh/oo•nah kah•bee•nah
How long is the crossing?	**Quanto dura la traversata?** _kwahn_•toh doo•rah lah trah•vehr•sah•tah

Genova, Livorno, Civitavecchia, Napoli, Messina and Reggio Calabria are the main ferry ports connecting the major and minor Italian islands. Travel along local coastal areas and lakes in Italy is enhanced by an extensive ferry system.

Taxi

Where can I get a taxi?	**Dove posso trovare un taxi?**
	doh•veh pohs•soh troh•vah•reh oon tah•ksee
Can you send a taxi?	**Posso avere un taxi?** _pohs•soh ah•veh•re oon tah•ksee_
Do you have the number for a taxi?	**Posso avere un numero per chiamare un taxi?**
	poh•soh ah•veh•reh oon noo•meh•roh pehr kyah•mah•reh oon tah•ksee
I'd like a taxi now/for tomorrow at (time)…	**Vorrei un taxi subito/domani alle…** _vohr•ray oon tah•ksee soo•bee•toh/doh•mah•nee ahl•leh…_
Pick me up at (place)…	**Venga a prendermi a…**
	vehn•gah ah prehn•dehr•mee ah…
I'm going to…	**Vado…** _vah•doh…_
this address	**a questo indirizzo** _ah kweh•stoh een•dee•ree•tsoh_
the airport	**all'aeroporto** _ahl•lah•eh•roh•pohr•toh_
the train [railway] station	**alla stazione ferroviaria** _ahl•lah stah•tsyoh•neh fehr•roh•vyah•ryah_
I'm late.	**Sono in ritardo.** _soh•noh een ree•tahr•doh_
Can you drive faster/slower?	**Può andare più velocemente/lentamente?** _pwoh ahn•dah•reh pyoo veh•loh•cheh•mehn•teh/ lehn•tah•mehn•teh_
Stop/Wait here.	**Si fermi/Mi aspetti qui.** _see fehr•mee/ mee ah•speht•tee kwee_
How much?	**Quant'è?** _kwahn•teh_

Get a taxi at taxi stands or reserve by phone; hailing a taxi in the street is not common. Extra charges are added for travel at night (10:00 p.m.–7:00 a.m.), on Sundays and holidays, for extra luggage and for trips outside of town. Tip the driver by rounding off to the nearest euro or two.

You said it would cost...	**Aveva detto che erano...** *ah·veh·vah deht·toh keh eh·rah·noh...*
Keep the change.	**Tenga il resto.** *tehn·gah eel reh·stoh*
A receipt, please.	**Una ricevuta, perfavore.** *oo·nah ree·cheh·voo·tah pehr fah·voh·re*

Bicycle & Motorbike

I'd like to hire...	**Vorrei noleggiare...** *vohr·ray noh·leh·djah·reh...*
a bicycle	**una bici** *oo·nah bee·chee*
a moped	**uno scooter** *oo·noh skoo·tehr*
a motorcycle	**una moto** *oo·nah moh·toh*
How much per day/week?	**Qual è la tariffa per un giorno/una settimana?** *kwah·leh lah tah·reef·fah pehr oon jyohr·noh/ oo·nah seht·tee·mah·nah*
Can I have a helmet/lock?	**Mi può dare un casco/lucchetto?** *mee pwoh dah·reh oon kah·skoh/look·keht·toh*

Car Hire

Where's the car rental [hire]?	**Dov'è un autonoleggio?** *doh·veh oon ow·toh·noh·leh·djoh*
I'd like...	**Vorrei...** *vohr·ray...*
a cheap/small car	**un'auto economica/piccola** *oo·now·toh eh·koh·noh·mee·kah/peek·koh·lah*
an automatic/ a manual	**un'auto con il cambio automatico/manuale** *oo·now·toh kohn eel kahm·byoh ow·toh·mah·tee·koh/ mah·nwah·leh*
air conditioning	**un'auto con l'aria condizionata** *oo·now·toh kohn lah·ryah kohn·dee·tsyoh·nah·tah*
a car seat	**un sedile** *oon seh·dee·leh*
How much...?	**Qual è la tariffa...?** *kwah·leh lah tah·reef·fah...*
per day/week	**per un giorno/una settimana** *pehr oon jyohr·noh/ oo·nah seht·tee·mah·nah*

YOU MAY HEAR...

Ha la patente internazionale? *ah lah pah•tehn•teh een•tehr•nah•tsyoh•nah•leh*	Do you have an international driver's license?
Il passaporto, per favore. *eel pahs•sah•pohr•toh pehr fah•voh•reh*	Your passport, please.
Desidera un'assicurazione supplementare? *deh•zee•deh•rah oo•nah•see•koo•rah•tsyoh•neh soop•pleh•mehn•tah•reh*	Do you want extra insurance?
Deve lasciare un deposito. *deh•veh lah•shah•reh oon deh•poh•zee•toh*	I'll need a deposit.
Metta le iniziali/Firmi qui. *meht•tah leh ee•nee•tsyah•lee/feer•mee kwee*	Initial/Sign here.

per kilometer	**a chilometro** *ah kee•loh•meh•troh*	
for unlimited mileage	**con chilometraggio illimitato** *kohn kee•loh•meh•trah•djoh eel•lee•mee•tah•toh*	
with insurance	**con l'assicurazione** *kohn l•ahs•see•koo•rah•tsyoh•neh*	
Are there discounts?	**Fate sconti?** *fah•teh skohn•tee*	

Fuel Station

Where's the fuel station?	**Dov'è un benzinaio?** *doh•veh oon behn•dzee•nah•yoh*
Fill it up.	**Faccia il pieno, per favore.** *fah•chyah eel pyeh•noh pehr fah•voh•reh*
...euros, please.	**...euro, per favore.** *...eh•oo•roh pehr fah•voh•reh*
I'll pay in cash/by credit card.	**Pago in contanti/con carta di credito.** *pah•goh een kohn•tahn•tee/kohn kahr•tah dee kreh•dee•toh*

YOU MAY SEE...

SUPER	super
PREMIUM	premium
DIESEL	diesel

Asking Directions

Is this the way to...?	**Vado bene per...?** _vah_·doh _beh_·neh pehr...
How far is it to...?	**Quanto dista...?** _kwahn_·toh _dees_·tah...
Where's...?	**Dov'è...?** doh·_veh_...
...Street	**Via...** _vee_·ah...
this address	**questo indirizzo** _kweh_·stoh een·dee·_ree_·tsoh

YOU MAY HEAR...

sempre dritto _sehm_·preh _dreet_·toh	straight ahead
a sinistra ah see·_nee_·strah	left
a destra ah _deh_·strah	right
all'angolo/dietro l'angolo	on the corner/around
ahl·_lahn_·goh·loh/_dyeh_·troh _lahn_·goh·loh	the corner
di fronte a dee _frohn_·teh ah	opposite
dietro a _dyeh_·troh ah	behind
accanto a ahk·_kahn_·toh ah	next to
dopo _doh_·poh	after
a nord/sud ah nohrd/sood	north/south
a est/ovest ah ehst/_oh_·vehst	east/west
al semaforo ahl seh·_mah_·foh·roh	at the traffic light
all'incrocio ahl·leen·_kroh_·chyoh	at the intersection

the highway [motorway]	**l'autostrada** /l·ow·toh·_strah_·dah
Can you show me on the map?	**Può indicarmelo sulla cartina?** _pwoh een·dee·_kahr_·meh·loh _sool_·lah kahr·_tee_·nah
I'm lost.	**Mi sono perso m/persa f.** mee _soh_·noh _pehr_·soh/_pehr_·sah

Parking

Can I park here?	**Posso parcheggiare qui?** _pohs_·soh pahr·keh·_djah_·reh kwee
Where's the parking lot [car park]/ parking meter?	**Dov'è il parcheggio/parchimetro?** doh·_veh_ eel pahr·_keh_·djoh/pahr·_kee_·meh·troh
How much...?	**Quanto costa...?** _kwahn_·toh _koh_·stah...
per hour	**all'ora** ahl·_loh_·rah
per day	**al giorno** ahl _jyohr_·noh
for overnight	**per tutta la notte** pehr _toot_·tah lah _noht_·teh

Breakdown & Repair

| My car broke down/ won't start. | **La mia auto ha un'avaria al motore/non parte.** lah _mee_·ah _ow_·toh ah oo·nah·vah·_ree_·ah ahl moh·_toh_·reh/nohn _pahr_·teh |
| Can you fix it (today)? | **Può ripararla (oggi)?** pwoh ree·pah·_rahr_·lah (_oh_·djee) |

Street parking in cities in limited; it's best to park in a **parcheggio** (parking lot or garage), day or night. Do not park in areas marked **Divieto di sosta** (no stopping except in emergency), **Divieto di fermata** (no stopping at any time) or **Passo carrabile** (do not block passageway).

YOU MAY SEE...

STOP	**STOP**	stop
▽	**DARE LA PRECEDENZA**	yield
●	**DIVIETO DI SOSTA**	no parking
⚠	**CURVA PERICOLOSA**	dangerous curve
←	**SENSO UNICO**	one way
○	**STRADA CHIUSA**	road closed
⊖	**DIVIETO DI SORPASSO**	no passing
⊘	**DIVIETO DI INVERSIONE DI MARCIA**	no u-turn

When will it be ready?	**Per quando è pronta?** *pehr kwahn•doh è prohn•tah*
How much?	**Quanto mi costa?** *kwahn•toh mee koh•stah*
I have a puncture/ flat tyre (tire).	**Ho una ruota bucata/sgonfia** *oh oo•nah roo•oh•tah boo•kah•tah/zgohn•fyah*

Accidents

There was an accident.	**C'è stato un incidente.** *cheh stah•toh oon een•chee•dehn•teh*
Call an ambulance/ the police.	**Chiami un'ambulanza/la polizia.** *kyah•mee oo•nahm•boo•lahn•tsah/lah poh•lee•tsee•ah*

Places to Stay

ESSENTIAL

Can you recommend a hotel?	**Può consigliarmi un hotel?** *pwoh kohn•see•<u>llyahr</u>•mee oon oh•<u>tehl</u>*
I have a reservation.	**Ho una prenotazione.** *oh <u>oo</u>•nah preh•noh•tah•<u>tsyoh</u>•neh*
My name is…	**Mi chiamo…** *mee <u>kyah</u>•moh…*
Do you have a room…?	**Avete una camera…?** *ah•<u>veh</u>•teh <u>oo</u>•nah <u>kah</u>•meh•rah…*
for one/two	**singola/doppia** *<u>seen</u>•goh•lah/<u>dohp</u>•pyah*
with a bathroom	**con bagno** *kohn <u>bah</u>•nyoh*
with air conditioning	**con aria condizionata** *kohn <u>ah</u>•ryah kohn•dee•tsyoh•<u>nah</u>•tah*
For…	**Per…** *pehr…*
tonight	**stanotte** *stah•<u>noht</u>•teh*
two nights	**due notti** *<u>doo</u>•eh <u>noht</u>•tee*
one week	**una settimana** *<u>oo</u>•nah seht•tee•<u>mah</u>•nah*
How much?	**Quanto costa?** *<u>kwahn</u>•toh <u>koh</u>•stah*
Is there anything cheaper?	**C'è qualcosa di più economico?** *cheh kwahl•<u>koh</u>•zah dee pyoo eh•koh•<u>noh</u>•mee•koh*
When's check-out?	**A che ora devo lasciare la camera?** *ah keh <u>oh</u>•rah <u>deh</u>•voh lah•<u>shah</u>•reh lah <u>kah</u>•meh•rah*
Can I leave this in the safe?	**Posso lasciare questo nella cassaforte?** *<u>pohs</u>•soh lah•<u>shah</u>•reh <u>kweh</u>•stoh <u>nehl</u>•lah kahs•sah•<u>fohr</u>•teh*
Can I leave my bags?	**Posso lasciare le valigie?** *<u>pohs</u>•soh lah•<u>shah</u>•reh leh vah•<u>lee</u>•jyeh*
I'd like the bill/receipt.	**Vorrei il conto/la ricevuta.** *<u>vohr</u>•ray eel <u>kohn</u>•toh/lah ree•cheh•<u>voo</u>•tah*

I'll pay in cash/ by credit card.	**Pago in contanti/con carta di credito.**
	pah·goh een kohn·tahn·tee/kohn kahr·tah dee kreh·dee·toh

Somewhere to Stay

Can you recommend...?	**Può consigliarmi...?** *pwoh kohn·see·llyahr·mee...*
a hotel	**un hotel** *oon oh·tehl*
a hostel	**un ostello** *oon oh·stehl·loh*
a campsite	**un campeggio** *oon kahm·peh·djoh*
a bed and breakfast	**una pensione** *oo·nah pehn·syoh·neh*
What is it near?	**Vicino cosa c'è?** *vee·chee·noh koh·zah cheh*
How do I get there?	**Come ci si arriva?** *koh·meh chee see ahr·ree·vah*

At the Hotel

I have a reservation.	**Ho una prenotazione.** *oh oo·nah preh·noh·tah·tsyoh·neh*
My name is...	**Mi chiamo...** *mee kyah·moh...*
Do you have a room...?	**Avete una camera...?** *ah·veh·teh oo·nah kah·meh·rah...*
with a bathroom [toilet]/shower	**con bagno/doccia** *kohn bah·nyoh/ doh·chyah*
with air conditioning	**con aria condizionata** *kohn ah·ryah kohn·dee·tsyoh·nah·tah*
that's smoking/ non-smoking	**per fumatori/non fumatori** *pehr foo·mah·toh·ree/nohn foo·mah·toh·ree*
For...	**Per...** *pehr...*
tonight	**stanotte** *stah·noht·teh*
two nights	**due notti** *doo·eh noht·tee*
a week	**una settimana** *oo·nah seht·tee·mah·nah*

If you didn't reserve accommodations before your trip, visit the local **l'ufficio informazioni turistiche**, tourist information office, for recommendations on places to stay.

Do you have…?	**C'è…?** *cheh…*
a computer	**un computer** *oon kohm·pyoo·tehr*
an elevator [lift]	**l'ascensore** *lah·shehn·soh·reh*
(wireless) internet service	**il collegamento Internet (wireless)** *eel kohl·leh·gah·mehn·toh een·tehr·neht (wyer·lehs)*
room service	**il servizio in camera** *eel sehr·vee·tsyoh een kah·meh·rah*
a pool	**la piscina** *lah pee·shee·nah*
a gym	**la palestra** *lah pah·leh·strah*
I need…	**Mi serve…** *mee sehr·veh…*
an extra bed	**un altro letto** *oon ahl·troh leht·toh*
a cot	**un lettino** *oon leht·tee·noh*
a crib	**una culla** *oo·nah kool·lah*

For Numbers, see page 167.

Price

How much per day/week?	**Quanto costa al giorno/alla settimana?** _kwahn•toh koh•stah ahl jyohr•noh/ahl•lah seht•tee•mah•nah_
Does that include breakfast/sales tax [VAT]?	**La prima colazione/L'IVA è inclusa?** _lah pree•mah koh•lah•tsyoh•neh/lee•vah eh een•kloo•sah_
Are there any discounts?	**Fate sconti?** _fah•teh skohn•tee_

Preferences

Can I see the room?	**Posso vedere la stanza?** _pohs•soh veh•deh•reh lah stahn•tsah_
I'd like a...room.	**Vorrei una...camera.** _vohr•ray oo•nah... kah•meh•rah_
better	**migliore** _mee•llyoh•reh_
bigger	**più grande** _pyoo grahn•deh_
cheaper	**più economica** _pyoo eh•koh•noh•mee•kah_
quieter	**più silenziosa/tranquilla** _pyoo see•lehn•tsyoh•sa/ trahn•kweehl•lah_
I'll take it.	**La prendo.** _lah prehn•doh_
No, I won't take it.	**Non la prendo.** _nohn lah prehn•doh_

A wide variety of accommodation is available in Italy, from budget to luxury. In recent years, **agriturismo** (farm-stays or ecotourism) have become very popular; these offer countryside locations, usually on a working farm, and often serve locally produced food. You may wish to stay in a **villa**, an upscale—and expensive—home or apartment, which often has a pool. **Una pensione** (bed and breakfast) is an ideal accommodation for budget-minded travelers who'd like to experience how Italians live. **Un hotel** can range in quality and price; many international chains have hotels throughout Italy.

YOU MAY HEAR...

Il suo passaporto/La sua carta di credito, per favore. *eel <u>soo</u>•oh pahs•sah•<u>pohr</u>•toh/lah <u>soo</u>•ah <u>kahr</u>•tah dee <u>kreh</u>•dee•toh pehr fah•<u>voh</u>•reh*

Your passport/credit card, please.

Compili questo modulo. *kohm•pee•lee <u>kweh</u>•stoh <u>moh</u>•doo•loh*

Fill out this form.

Firmi qui. *<u>feer</u>•mee kwee*

Sign here.

Questions

Where's...?	**Dov'è...?** *doh•<u>veh</u>...*
the bar	**il bar** *eel bahr*
the toilet	**la toilette** *lah <u>twah</u>•leht*
the elevator [lift]	**l'ascensore** *lah•shehn•<u>soh</u>•reh*
Can I have...?	**Può darmi...?** *pwoh <u>dahr</u>•mee...*
a blanket	**una coperta** *<u>oo</u>•nah koh•<u>pehr</u>•tah*
an iron	**un ferro da stiro** *oon <u>fehr</u>•roh dah <u>stee</u>•roh*
a pillow	**un cuscino** *oon koo•<u>shee</u>•noh*
soap	**una saponetta** *<u>oo</u>•nah sah•poh•<u>neht</u>•tah*
the room key/ key card	**la chiave/la chiave magnetica della camera** *lah kyah•veh/lah kyah•veh mah•nyeh•tee•kah dehl•lah kah•meh•rah*
toilet paper	**della carta igienica** *<u>dehl</u>•lah <u>kahr</u>•tah ee•<u>jyeh</u>•nee•kah*
a towel	**un asciugamano** *oon ah•shoo•gah•<u>mah</u>•noh*
Do you have an adapter for this?	**Avete un adattatore?** *ah•<u>veh</u>•teh oon ah•daht•toh•<u>tohr</u>•eh*
How do I turn on the lights?	**Come si accendono le luci?** *<u>koh</u>•meh see ah•<u>chehn</u>•doh•noh leh <u>loo</u>•chee*
Can you wake me at...?	**Può svegliarmi alle...?** *pwoh zveh•<u>llyahr</u>•mee <u>ahl</u>•leh...*

Can I leave this in the safe?	**Posso lasciare questo nella cassaforte?** _pohs•soh lah•shah•reh kweh•stoh nehl•lah kahs•sah•fohr•teh_
Can I have my things from the safe?	**Posso prendere le mie cose dalla cassaforte?** _pohs•soh prehn•deh•reh leh mee•eh koh•zeh dahl•lah kahs•sah•fohr•teh_
Is there mail [post]/ a message for me?	**C'è posta/Ci sono messaggi per me?** _cheh poh•stah/chee soh•noh mehs•sah•djee pehr meh_
Do you have a laundry service?	**Fate servizio di lavanderia?** _fah•teh sehr•vee•tsyohdee lah•vahn•deh•ree•ah_

Problems

There's a problem.	**C'è un problema.** _cheh oon proh•bleh•mah_
I lost my key/key card.	**Ho perso la chiave/chiave elettronica.** _oh pehr•soh lah kyah•veh/kyah•veh eh•leht•troh•nee•kah_
I'm locked out of the room.	**Sono rimasto chiuso?/rimasta chiusa/fuori.** _soh•noh ree•mah•stoh kyoo•zoh?/ree•mah•stah kyoo•zah/fwoh•ree_
There's no hot water/toilet paper.	**Non c'è acqua calda/carta igienica.** _nohn cheh ah•kwah kahl•dah/kahr•tah ee•jyeh•nee•kah_
The room is dirty.	**La camera è sporca.** _lah kah•meh•rah eh spohr•kah_
There are bugs in the room.	**In camera ci sono degli insetti.** _een kah•meh•rah chee soh•noh deh•llyee een•seht•tee_
The…doesn't work.	**…non funziona.** _…nohn foon•tsyoh•nah_
Can you fix…?	**Può riparare…?** _pwoh ree•pah•rah•reh…_
the air conditioning	**l'aria condizionata** _lah•ryah kohn•dee•tsyoh•nah•tah_
the fan	**il ventilatore** _eel vehn•tee•lah•toh•reh_
the heat [heating]	**il riscaldamento** _eel ree•skahl•dah•mehn•toh_
the light	**la luce** _lah loo•cheh_
the TV	**la TV** _lah tee•voo_
the toilet	**il gabinetto** _eel gah•bee•neht•toh_
I'd like another room.	**Vorrei un'altra camera.** _vohr•ray oo•nahl•trah kah•meh•rah_

YOU MAY SEE…

SPINGERE/TIRARE	push/pull
TOILETTE	bathroom [toilet]
DOCCIA	shower
ASCENSORE	elevator [lift]
SCALE	stairs
LAVANDERIA	laundry
NON DISTURBARE	do not disturb
PORTA ANTINCENDIO	fire door
USCITA (D'EMERGENZA)	(emergency) exit
SERVIZIO SVEGLIA	wake-up call

Checking Out

When's check-out?	**A che ora devo lasciare la camera?** _ah keh oh•rah deh•voh lah•shah•reh lah kah•meh•rah_
Can I leave my bags here until…?	**Posso lasciare le valigie fino alle…?** _pohs•soh lah•shah•reh leh vah•lee•jyeh fee•noh ahl•leh…_
Can I have an itemized bill/receipt?	**Posso avere il conto dettagliato/la ricevuta?** _pohs•soh ah•veh•reh eel kohn•toh deht•tah•llyah•toh/ lah ree•cheh•voo•tah_
I think there's a mistake.	**Credo che ci sia un errore.** _kreh•doh keh chee see•ah oon ehr•roh•reh_
I'll pay in cash/by credit card.	**Pago in contanti/con carta di credito.** _pah•ghoh een kohn•tahn•tee/kohn kahr•tah dee kreh•dee•toh_

Voltage is 220–240V, and plugs are two-pronged. You may need a converter and/or an adapter for your appliances.

A service fee is generally included in bills throughout Italy. It's optional to tip porters and housekeeping staff, though a tip for good service is always appreciated. Your concierge will appreciate a tip for any helpful services provided.

Renting

I reserved an apartment/a room.	**Ho prenotato un appartamento/una camera.** *oh preh·noh·tah·toh oon ahp·pahr·tah·mehn·toh/ oo·nah kah·meh·rah*
My name is…	**Mi chiamo…** *mee kyah·moh…*
Can I have the key/key card?	**Mi può dare la chiave/chiave elettronica?** *mee pwoo dah·reh lah kyah·veh/kyah·veh eh·leht·troh·nee·kah*
Are there…?	**Ci sono…?** *chee soh·noh…*
dishes	**i piatti** *ee pyaht·tee*
pillows	**i cuscini** *ee koo·shee·nee*
sheets	**le lenzuola** *leh lehn·tswoh·lah*
towels	**gli asciugamani** *llyee ah·shoo·gah·mah·nee*
kitchen utensils	**gli utensili** *llyee oo·tehn·see·lee*
When do I put out the bins/ recycling?	**Quando si mette fuori il secchio della spazzatura/il riciclaggio?** *kwahn·doh see meht·teh fwoh·ree eel sehk·kyoh dehl·lah spah·tsah·too·rah/ eel ree·chee·klah·djoh*
…is broken.	**…non funziona.** *…nohn foon·tsyoh·nah*
How does…work?	**Come funziona…?** *koh·meh foon·tsyoh·nah…*
the air conditioner	**il condizionatore** *eel kohn·dee·tsyoh·nah·toh·reh*
the dishwasher	**la lavastoviglie** *lah lah·vah·stoh·vee·llyeh*
the freezer	**il freezer** *eel free·zehr*
the heater	**il riscaldamento** *eel ree·skahl·dah·mehn·toh*
the microwave	**il microonde** *eel mee·kroh·ohn·deh*

the refrigerator	**il frigo** *eel free·goh*
the stove	**la cucina** *lah koo·chee·nah*
the washing machine	**la lavatrice** *lah lah·vah·tree·cheh*

Domestic Items

I need...	**Ho bisogno di...** *oh bee·soh·nyoh dee...*
an adapter	**un adattatore** *oon ah·daht·toh·toh·reh*
aluminum [kitchen] foil	**carta stagnola** *kahr·tah stah·nyoh·lah*
a bottle opener	**un apribottiglie** *oon ah·pree·boht·tee·llyeh*
a broom	**una scopa** *oo·nah skoh·pah*
a can opener	**un apriscatole** *oon ah·pree·skah·toh·leh*
cleaning supplies	**prodotti per le pulizie** *proh·doht·tee pehr leh poo·lee·tsee·eh*
a corkscrew	**un cavatappi** *oon kah·vah·tahp·pee*
detergent	**detersivo** *deh·tehr·see·voh*
dishwashing liquid	**detersivo per i piatti** *deh·tehr·see·voh pehr ee pyaht·tee*
bin bags	**sacchetti per i rifiuti** *sahk·keht·tee pehr ee ree·fyoo·tee*
a lightbulb	**una lampadina** *oo·nah lahm·pah·dee·nah*
matches	**fiammiferi** *fyahm·mee·feh·ree*

a mop	**un mocio** *oon <u>moh</u>•choh*
napkins	**tovaglioli** *toh•vah•<u>llyoh</u>•lee*
paper towels	**carta da cucina** *<u>kahr</u>•tah dah koo•<u>chee</u>•nah*
plastic wrap	**pellicola per alimenti** *pehl•<u>lee</u>•koh•lah*
[cling film]	*pehr ah•lee•<u>mehn</u>•tee*
a plunger	**uno sturalavandini** *<u>oo</u>•noh stoo•rah•lah•vahn•<u>dee</u>•nee*
scissors	**un paio di forbici** *oon <u>pah</u>•yoh dee <u>fohr</u>•bee•chee*
a vacuum cleaner	**un aspirapolvere** *oon ah•spee•rah•<u>pohl</u>•veh•reh*

For In the Kitchen, see page 78.

For Conversion Tables, see page 172.

At the Hostel

Is there a bed available?	**C'è un letto disponibile?** *cheh oon <u>leht</u>•toh dee•spoh•<u>nee</u>•bee•leh*
Can I have…?	**Potrei avere…?** *poh•<u>tray</u> ah•<u>veh</u>•reh*
a single/double room	**una camera singola/doppia** *<u>oo</u>•nah <u>kah</u>•meh•rah <u>seen</u>•goh•lah/<u>dohp</u>•pyah*
a blanket	**una coperta** *<u>oo</u>•nah koh•<u>pehr</u>•tah*
a pillow	**un cuscino** *oon koo•<u>shee</u>•noh*
sheets	**delle lenzuola** *<u>dehl</u>•leh lehn•<u>tswoh</u>•lah*
a towel	**un asciugamano** *oon ah•shoo•gah•<u>mah</u>•noh*

Hostels are inexpensive accommodations that have dormitory-style sleeping arrangements and private or semi-private rooms. Some hostels have rooms with private bathrooms, though most offer shared bathrooms. There is usually a self-service kitchen on site. Reservations are recommended in advance in larger cities and popular tourist destinations during the tourist season. Visit the Hosteling International website for details.

Do you have lockers?	**Avete gli armadietti col lucchetto?** *ah·veh·the llyee ahr·mah·dyeht·tee khol look·keht·toh*
When do you lock up?	**A che ora chiudete?** *ah keh oh·rah kyoo·deh·teh*
Do I need a membership card?	**Ci vuole la tessera di iscrizione?** *chee vwoh·leh lah teh·seh·rah deehs·kree·tsyoh·neh*
Here's my international student card.	**Ecco la mia tessera studentesca internazionale.** *ehk·koh lah mee·ah teh·seh·rah stoo·dehn·tehs·kah een·tehr·nah·tsyoh·nah·leh*

Going Camping

Can I camp here?	**Si può campeggiare?** *see pwoh kahm·peh·djah·reh*
Where's the campsite?	**Dov'è il campeggio?** *doh·veh eel kahm·peh·djoh*
What is the charge per day/week?	**Qual è la tariffa per un giorno/una settimana?** *kwah·leh lah tah·reef·fah pehr oon jyohr·noh/ oo·nah seht·tee·mah·nah*
Are there...?	**Ci sono...?** *chee soh·noh...*
cooking facilities	**le attrezzature per cucinare** *leh aht·treh·tsah·too·reh pehr koo·chee·nah·reh*
electric outlets	**le prese elettriche** *leh preh·seh eh·leht·tree·keh*
laundry facilities	**le lavanderie** *leh lah·vahn·deh·ree·eh*
showers	**le docce** *leh doh·cheh*
tents for rent [hire]	**tende a noleggio** *tehn·deh ah noh·leh·djoh*

YOU MAY SEE...

ACQUA POTABILE	drinking water
NO CAMPING	no camping
DIVIETO DI FALÒ/BARBECUE	no fires/barbecues

Where can I empty the chemical toilet? **Dove posso vuotare il water?** _doh•veh pohs•soh vwoh•tah•reh eel vah•tehr_

For Domestic Items, see page 44.

For In the Kitchen, see page 78.

Communications

ESSENTIAL

Where's an internet cafe? **Dov'è un Internet caffè?** _doh•veh oon een•tehr•neht kahf•feh_

Can I access the internet/check e-mail? **Posso collegarmi a Internet/controllare le e-mail?** _pohs•soh kohl•leh•gahr•mee ah een•tehr•neht/kohn•trohl•lah•reh leh ee•mayl_

How much per hour/half hour? **Quanto costa per un'ora/mezz'ora?** _kwahn•toh koh•stah pehr oon•oh•rah/mehdz•oh•rah_

How do I log on? **Come si fa il login?** _koh•meh see fah eel loh•geen_

A phone card, please. **Una scheda telefonica, per favore.** _oo•nah skeh•dah teh•leh•foh•nee•kah pehr fah•voh•reh_

Can I have your number, please? **Mi può dare il suo numero, per favore?** _mee pwoh dah•reh eel soo•oh noo•meh•roh pehr fah•voh•reh_

Here's my number/e-mail. **Ecco il mio numero/la mia e-mail.** _ehk•koh eel mee•oh noo•meh•roh/lah mee•ah ee•mayl_

Call/E-mail me. **Mi chiami/mandi una e-mail.** _mee kyah•mee/mahn•dee oo•nah ee•mayl_

Hello. This is… **Pronto. Sono…** _prohn•toh soh•noh…_

Can I speak to…? **Posso parlare con…?** _pohs•soh pahr•lah•reh kohn…_

Can you repeat that? **Può ripetere?** _pwoh ree•peh•teh•reh_

I'll call back later. **Richiamo più tardi.** _ree•kyah•moh pyoo tahr•dee_

Bye.	**Arrivederla.** ahr·ree·veh·_dehr_·lah
Where's the post office?	**Dov'è un ufficio postale?** doh·_veh_ oon oof·_fee_·chyoh poh·_stah_·leh
I'd like to send this to…	**Vorrei inviare questo a…** vohr·_ray_ een·_vyah_·reh _kweh_·stoh ah…

Online

Where's an internet cafe?	**Dov'è un Internet caffè?** doh·_veh_ oon _een_·tehr·neht kahf·_feh_
Does it have wireless internet?	**C'è il wireless?** cheh eel _wyehr_·lehs
What is the WiFi password?	**Qual è la password Wi-Fi?** koo·_ahl_·eh lah pahs·_swoh_·rd wah·ee fah·ee
Is the WiFi free?	**Il WiFi è gratis?** eel wah·ee fah·ee eh grah·tees
Do you have bluetooth?	**Avete il Bluetooth?** ah·_veh_·teh eel bloo·too·th
How do I turn the computer on/off?	**Come si accende/spegne il computer?** _koh_·meh see ah·_chehn_·deh/_speh_·nyeh eel kohm·_pyoo_·tehr
Can I…?	**Posso…?** _pohs_·soh…
access the internet	**collegarmi (a Internet)** kohl·leh·_gahr_·mee (ah _een_·tehr·neht)
check e-mail	**controllare le e-mail** kohn·trohl·_lah_·reh leh _ee_·mayl
print	**stampare** stahm·_pah_·reh
plug in/charge my laptop/iPhone/ iPad/BlackBerry?	**collegare/ricaricare il mio portatile/iPhone/iPad?** kohl·leh·_gah_·reh eel mee·oh pohr·tah·tee·leh/ahy·fon/ ahy·pad
access Skype?	**usare Skype?** oo·_sah_·reh skah·eep

How much per hour/half hour?	**Quanto costa per un'ora/mezz'ora?** _kwahn·toh koh·stah pehr oon·oh·rah/mehdz·oh·rah_
How do I…?	**Come…?** _koh·meh…_
connect/ disconnect	**ci si collega/scollega** _chee see kohl·leh·gah/ skohl·leh·gah_
log on/log off	**si fa il login/logout** _see fah eel loh·geen/loh·gowt_
type this symbol	**digiti questo simbolo** _dee·jee·tee kweh·stoh seem·boh·loh_
What's your e-mail?	**Qual è la sua e-mail?** _kwahl·eh lah soo·ah ee-mayl_
My e-mail is…	**La mia e-mail è…** _lah mee·ah ee-mayl eh…_
Do you have a scanner?	**Avete uno scanner?** _ah·veh·teh oo·noh skahn·nehr_

Social Media

Are you on Facebook/ Twitter?	**È su Facebook/Twitter?** *(polite form)* _eh soo feh·eez·book/tweet·tehr_
	Sei su Facebook/Twitter? *(informal form)* _seh·ee soo feh·eez·book/tweet·tehr_
What's your user name?	**Qual è il suo nome utente?** *(polite form)* _koo·ahl eh eel soo·oh noh·meh oo·tehn·teh_
	Qual è il tuo nome utente? *(informal form)* _Koo·ahl·eh eel too·oh noh·meh oo·tehn·teh_

I'll add you as a friend.	**La aggiungerò come amico.** *(polite form)*
	lah ah•djoon•djeh•roh koh•meh ah•mee•koh
	Ti aggiungerò come amico. *(informal form)*
	tee ah•djoon•djeh•roh koh•meh ah•mee•koh
I'll follow you Twitter.	**La seguirò su Twitter.** *(polite form)* *lah*
	seh•gwee•roh soo tweet•tehr
	Ti seguirò su Twitter. *(informal form)* *tee*
	seh•gwee•roh soo tweet•tehr
Are you following...?	**Segue...?** *(polite form)* *seh•gweh...*
	Seguite...? *(informal form)* *seh•gwee•teh...*
I'll put the pictures on Facebook/Twitter.	**Metterò le foto su Facebook/Twitter.**
	meht•teh•roh leh foh•toh soo feh•eez•book/tweet•tehr

YOU MAY SEE...

CHIUDI	close
ELIMINA	delete
E-MAIL	e-mail
ESCI	exit
AIUTO	help
INSTANT MESSENGER	instant messenger
INTERNET	internet
LOGIN	login
NUOVO (MESSAGGIO)	new (message)
ACCESSO/SPENTO	on/off
APRI	open
STAMPA	print
SALVA	save
INVIA	send
NOME UTENTE/PASSWORD	username/password
WIRELESS	wireless internet

I'll tag you in the pictures.	**La taggherò nelle foto.** *(polite form)* *lah tahg·gheh·roh nehl·leh foh·toh* **Ti taggherò nelle foto.** *(informal form)* *tee tahg·gheh·roh nehl·leh foh·toh*

Phone

A phone card/prepaid phone please.	**Una scheda telefonica/ telefonoprepagato, per favore.** *oo·nah skeh·dah teh·leh·foh·nee·kah/ teh·leh·foh·noh preh·pah·gah·toh pehr fah·voh·reh*
How much?	**Quant'è?** *kwahn·teh*
Where's the pay phone?	**Dove posso trovare un telefono pubblico/ una cabina telefonica?** *doh·veh pohs·soh troh·vah·reh oon teh·leh·foh·noh puhb·blee·koh/ oo·nah kah·bee·nah teh·leh·foh·nee·kah*
What's the area code/country code for...?	**Qual è il prefisso/prefisso internazionale per...?** *kwahl eh eel preh·fees·soh/preh·fees·soh een·tehr·nah·tsyoh·nah·leh pehr...*
What's the number for Information?	**Che numero ha il servizio informazioni?** *keh noo·meh·roh ah eel sehr·vee·tsyoh een·fohr·mah·tsyoh·nee*
I'd like the number for...	**Vorrei il numero di/del/della/dell'...** *vohr·ray eel noo·meh·roh pehr dee/dehl/dehl·lah/dehl...*
I'd like to call collect [reverse the charges].	**Vorrei fare una telefonata a carico del destinatario.** *vohr·ray fah·reh oo·nah teh·leh·foh·nah·tah ah kah·ree·koh dehl deh·stee·nah·tah·ryoh*
My phone doesn't work here.	**Il telefonino non prende.** *eel teh·leh·foh·nee·noh nohn prehn·deh*
What network are you on?	**Su quale rete siamo?** *soo koo·ah·leh reh·teh syah·moh*

Is it 3G?	**È una rete 3G?** eh oo·nah reh·teh treh djee
I have run out of credit/minutes.	**Non ho più credito/minuti.** nohn oh pyoo kreh·dee·toh/mee·noo·tee
Can I buy some credit?	**Posso acquistare una ricarica?** pohs·soh ah·kwee·stah·reh oo·nah ree·kah·ree·kah
Do you have a phone charger?	**Avete un caricabatterie per il telefono?** ah·veh·teh oon kah·ree·kah·baht·teh·ree·eh pehr eel teh·leh·foh·noh
Can I have your number, please?	**Mi può dare il suo numero, per favore?** mee pwoh dah·reh eel soo·oh noo·meh·roh pehr fah·voh·reh

YOU MAY HEAR...

Chi parla? kee pahr·lah	Who's calling?
Attenda. aht·tehn·dah	Hold on.
Le passo il numero. leh pahs·soh eel noo·meh·roh	I'll put you through.
Non c'è. nohn cheh	He/She is not here.
È al telefono. eh ahl teh·leh·foh·noh	He/She is on another line.
Vuole lasciare un messaggio? vwoh·leh lah·shah·reh oon mehs·sah·djoh	Would you like to leave a message?
Richiami più tardi/fra dieci minuti. ree·kyah·mee pyoo tahr·dee/frah dyeh·chee mee·noo·tee	Call back later/in 10 minutes.
Può richiamarla? pwoh ree·kyah·mahr·lah	Can he/she call you back?
Mi lascia il suo numero? mee lah·shah eel soo·oh noo·meh·roh	What's your number?

Most public phones are card-operated; phone cards can be purchased at **edicole** (newsstands), **caffè** (coffee bars) and **tabacchi** (tobacconists). For international calls, calling cards are the most economical. Calling internationally from your hotel may be convenient, but the rates can be very expensive.

To call the U.S. or Canada from Italy, dial 001 + area code + phone number. To call the U.K. from Italy, dial 0044 + area code (minus the first 0) + phone number.

To make a local or national call within Italy, dial the area code then the phone number. A list of codes can be found in the phone book.

Here's my number.	**Ecco il mio numero.** *ehk•koh eel mee•oh noo•meh•roh*
Call/Text me.	**Mi chiami/mandi un SMS.** *mee kyah•mee/ mahn•dee oon ehs•seh ehm•meh ehs•seh*
I'll call you.	**La chiamo.** *lah kyah•moh*
I'll text you.	**Le mando un SMS.** *leh mahn•doh oon ehs•seh ehm•meh ehs•seh*

For Grammar, see page 162.

For Numbers, see page 167.

Telephone Etiquette

Hello. This is...	**Pronto. Sono...** *prohn•toh soh•noh...*
Can I speak to...?	**Posso parlare con...?** *pohs•soh pahr•lah•reh kohn...*
Extension...	**Interno...** *een•tehr•noh...*
Speak louder/more slowly, please.	**Parli più forte/lentamente, per favore.** *pahr•lee pyoo fohr•teh/lehn•tah•mehn•teh pehr fah•voh•reh*

Can you repeat that?	**Può ripetere?** *pwoh ree•peh•teh•reh*
I'll call back later.	**Richiamo più tardi.** *ree•kyah•moh pyoo tahr•dee*
Bye.	**Arrivederla.** *ahr•ree•veh•dehr•lah*

For Business Travel, see page 141.

Fax

Can I send/receive a fax here?	**Posso inviare/ricevere un fax?** *pohs•soh een•vyah•reh/ree•cheh•veh•reh oon fahks*
What's the fax number?	**Qual è il numero di fax?** *kwahl•eh eel noo•meh•roh dee fahks*
Please fax this to...	**Invii questo fax a..., per favore.** *een•vee•ee kweh•stoh fahks ah... pehr fah•voh•reh*

YOU MAY HEAR...

Riempia il modulo per la dogana. *ryehm•pee•ah eel moh•doo•loh pehr lah doh•gah•nah*	Fill out the customs declaration form.
Valore? *vah•loh•reh*	What's the value?
Cosa c'è dentro? *koh•zah cheh dehn•troh*	What's inside?

Post

Where's the post office/mailbox [postbox]?	**Dov'è un ufficio postale/una buca delle lettere?** doh·_veh_ oon oof·_fee_·chyoh poh·_stah_·leh/_oo_·nah _boo_·kah dehl·leh _leht_·teh·reh
A stamp for this postcard/letter to…	**Un francobollo per questa cartolina/ lettera per…** oon frahn·koh·_bohl_·loh pehr _kweh_·stah kahr·toh·_lee_·nah/_leht_·teh·rah pehr…
How much?	**Quant'è?** kwahn·_teh_
Send this package by airmail/express.	**Mandi questo pacco per posta aerea/ espresso.** _mahn_·dee _kweh_·stoh _pahk_·koh pehr _poh_·stah ah·_eh_·reh·ah/eh·_sprehs_·soh
A receipt, please.	**La ricevuta, per favore.** lah ree·cheh·_voo_·tah pehr fah·_voh_·reh

Food & Drink

Eating Out	57
Meals & Cooking	65
Drinks	80
On the Menu	85

ESSENTIAL

Can you recommend a good restaurant/ bar?	**Può consigliarmi un buon ristorante/bar?** pwoh kohn•see•_llyahr_•mee oon bwohn ree•stoh•_rahn_•teh/bahr
Is there a traditional/ an inexpensive restaurant nearby?	**C'è un ristorante tipico/economico qui vicino?** cheh oon ree•stoh•_rahn_•teh _tee_•pee•koh/ eh•koh•_noh_•mee•koh kwee vee•_chee_•noh
A table for..., please.	**Un tavolo per..., per favore.** oon _tah_•voh•loh pehr... pehr fah•_voh_•reh
Can we sit...?	**Possiamo sederci...?** pohs•_syah_•moh seh•_dehr_•chee...
here/there	**qui/là** kwee/lah
outside	**fuori** _fwoh_•ree
in a (non-) smoking area	**in una sala per (non) fumatori** een _oo_•nah sah•lah pehr (nohn) foo•mah•_toh_•ree
I'm waiting for someone.	**Sto aspettando qualcuno.** stoh ah•speht•_tahn_•doh kwahl•_koo_•noh
Where are the toilets?	**Dov'è la toilette?** doh•_veh_ lah twah•leht
The menu, please.	**Il menù, per favore.** eel meh•_noo_ pehr fah•_voh_•reh
What do you recommend?	**Cosa mi consiglia?** _koh_•zah mee kohn•_see_•llyah
I'd like...	**Vorrei...** vohr•_ray_...
Some more ..., please.	**Un po' di più..., per favore** oon poh dee pyoo, pehr fah•_voh_•reh
Enjoy your meal!	**Buon appetito!** bwohn ahp•peh•_tee_•toh
The check [bill], please.	**Il conto, per favore.** eel _kohn_•toh pehr fah•_voh_•reh

Is service included?	**Il servizio è compreso?** *eel sehr·<u>vee</u>·tsyoh eh kohm·<u>preh</u>·zoh*
Can I pay by credit card/have a receipt?	**Posso pagare con carta di credito/avere una ricevuta?** *pohs·soh pah·<u>gah</u>·reh kohn <u>kahr</u>·tah dee <u>kreh</u>·dee·toh/ah·<u>veh</u>·reh <u>oo</u>·nah ree·cheh·<u>voo</u>·tah*
Thank you!	**Grazie!** *<u>grah</u>·tsyeh*

Where to Eat

Can you recommend…?	**Può consigliarmi…?** *pwoh kohn·see·<u>llyahr</u>·mee…*
a restaurant	**un ristorante** *oon ree·stoh·<u>rahn</u>·teh*
a bar	**un bar** *oon bahr*
a cafe	**un caffè** *oon kahf·<u>feh</u>*
a fast-food place	**un fast food** *oon fahst food*
a pizzeria	**una pizzeria** *<u>oo</u>·nah pee·tseh·<u>ree</u>·ah*
a cheap restaurant	**un ristorante economico** *oon ree·stoh·rahn·teh eh·koh·noh·mee·koh*
an expensive restaurant	**un ristorante costoso/caro** *oon ree·stoh·rahn·teh kohs·toh·zoh/kah·roh*
a restaurant with a good view	**un ristorante con una bella vista/un bel panorama** *oon ree·stoh·rahn·teh kohn oo·nah behl·lah vees·tah/oon behl pah·noh·rah·mah*
an authentic/ a non-touristy restaurant	**un ristorante tradizionale/non turistico** *oon ree·stoh·rahn·teh trah·dee·tsyoh·nah·leh/ nohn too·rees·tee·koh*

Reservations & Preferences

We have a reservation.	**Abbiamo prenotato.** *ahb·<u>byah</u>·moh preh·noh·<u>tah</u>·toh*
My name is…	**Mi chiamo…** *mee <u>kyah</u>·moh…*

I'd like to reserve a table...	**Vorrei prenotare un tavolo...** *vohr•ray preh•noh•tah•reh oon tah•voh•loh...*
for two	**per due** *pehr doo•eh*
for this evening	**per questa sera** *pehr kweh•stah seh•rah*
for tomorrow at...	**per domani alle...** *pehr doh•mah•nee ahl•leh...*
A table for two, please.	**Un tavolo per due, per favore.** *oon tah•voh•loh pehr doo•eh pehr fah•voh•reh*
Can we sit...?	**Possiamo sederci...** *pohs•syah•moh seh•dehr•chee...*
here/there	**qui/là** *kwee/lah*
outside	**fuori** *fwoh•ree*
in a (non-) smoking area	**in una sala per (non) fumatori** *een oo•nah sah•lah pehr (nohn) foo•mah•toh•ree*

La prima colazione (breakfast) is typically espresso or cappuccino with a croissant or sweet pastry. **Il pranzo** (lunch) is served between 12:00 p.m. and 2:00 p.m. and is usually the main meal of the day. **La cena** (dinner) is served between 7:00 p.m. and 10:00 p.m. **Le merende** (snacks) are popular at mid-morning or mid-afternoon; these include a sweet pastry, ice cream or small pizza.

YOU MAY HEAR...

Ha prenotato?	Do you have
ah preh·noh·tah·toh	a reservation?
Per quante persone?	How many?
pehr kwahn·teh pehr·soh·neh	
Volete ordinare?	Are you ready
to voh·leh·teh ohr·dee·nah·reh	order?
Che cosa desidera?	What would you like?
keh koh·zah deh·zee·deh·rah	
Le consiglio... *leh kohn·see·llyoh...*	I recommend...
Buon appetito. *bwohn ahp·peh·tee·toh*	Enjoy your meal.

by the window	**vicino alla finestra** *vee·chee·noh ahl·lah fee·neh·strah*
in the shade	**all'ombra** *ahl·lohm·brah*
in the sun	**al sole** *ahl soh·leh*
Where are	**Dov'è la toilette?**
the toilets?	*doh·veh lah twah·leht*

How to Order

Excuse me!	**Scusi!** *skooh·see*
We're ready	**Vorremmo ordinare.** *vohr·rehm·moh*
to order.	*ohr·dee·nah·reh*
May I see the	**La carta dei vini, per favore.** *lah kahr·tah day*
wine list?	*vee·nee pehr fah·voh·reh*
I'd like...	**Vorrei...** *vohr·ray...*
a bottle of...	**una bottiglia di...** *oo·nah boht·tee·llyah dee...*
a carafe of...	**una caraffa di...** *oo·nah kah·rahf·fah dee...*
a glass of...	**un bicchiere di...** *oon beek·kyeh·reh dee...*
Can I have a menu?	**Il menù, per favore.** *eel meh·noo pehr fah·voh·reh*

Do you have…?	**Avete…?** ah·_veh_·teh…
a menu in English	**un menù in inglese** oon meh·_noo_ een een·_gleh_·zeh
a fixed-price menu	**un menù a prezzo fisso** oon meh·_noo_ ah _preh_·tsoh _fees_·soh
a children's menu	**un menù per bambini** oon meh·_noo_ pehr bahm·_bee_·nee
What do you recommend?	**Cosa mi consiglia?** _koh_·zah mee kohn·_see_·llyah
What's this?	**Questo che cos'è?** _kweh_·stoh keh koh·_zeh_
What's in it?	**Cosa c'è dentro?** _koh_·zah cheh _dehn_·troh
Is it spicy?	**È piccante?** eh peek·_kahn_·the
I'd like…	**Vorrei…** vohr·ray…
More…	**Dell'altro m /altra f …** dehl·_lahl_·troh/lahl·_trah_…
With/Without…	**Con/Senza…** kohn/sehn·tsah…
I can't have…	**Non posso mangiare…** nohn pohs·soh mahn·jyah·reh…
rare	**al sangue** ahl sahn·gweh
medium	**mediamente cotta** meh·dyah·mehn·teh koht·tah
well-done	**ben cotta** behn koht·tah
It's to go [take away].	**È da portare via.** eh dah pohr·_tahr_·eh _vee_·ah

For Drinks, see page 80.

YOU MAY SEE…

COPERTO	cover charge
PREZZO FISSO	fixed-price
MENÙ	menu
MENÙ DEL GIORNO	menu of the day
SERVIZIO (NON) COMPRESO	service (not) included
SPECIALITÀ DEL GIORNO	daily specials

Cooking Methods

baked	**al forno** *ahl _fohr_·noh*
boiled	**lesso** *_lehs_·soh*
braised	**brasato** *brah·_zah_·toh*
breaded	**impanato** *eem·pah·_nah_·toh*
creamed	**passato** *pahs·_sah_·toh*
diced	**a cubetti** *ah koo·_beht_·tee*
filleted	**filetto** *fee·_leht_·toh*
fried	**fritto** *_freet_·toh*
grilled	**grigliato** *gree·_llyah_·toh*
poached	**in bianco** *een _byahn_·koh*
roasted	**arrosto** *ahr·_roh_·stoh*
sautéed	**saltato** *sahl·_tah_·toh*
smoked	**affumicato** *ahf·foo·mee·_kah_·toh*
steamed	**al vapore** *ahl vah·_poh_·reh*
stewed	**stufato** *stoo·_fah_·toh*
stuffed	**ripieno** *ree·_pyeh_·noh*

Dietary Requirements

I'm...	**Sono...** *_soh_·noh...*
diabetic	**diabetico m /diabetica f** *dyah·_beh_·tee·koh/ dyah·_beh_·tee·kah*
lactose intolerant	**intollerante al lattosio** *een·tohl·leh·_rahn_·the ahl laht·_toh_·syoh*
vegetarian	**vegetariano m /vegetariana f** *veh·jeh·tah·_ryah_·noh/veh·jeh·tah·_ryah_·nah*
vegan	**vegano m /vegana f** *veh·_gah_·noh/veh·_gah_·nah*
I'm allergic to...	**Sono allergico m /allergica f a...** *_soh_·noh ahl·_lehr_·jee·koh/ahl·_lehr_·jee·kah ah...*
I can't eat...	**Non posso mangiare...** *nohn _pohs_·soh mahn·_jyah_·reh...*
dairy products	**i latticini** *ee laht·tee·_chee_·nee*

gluten	**il glutine** *eel gloo·tee·neh*
nuts	**le noci** *leh noh·chee*
pork	**il maiale** *eel mah·yah·leh*
shellfish	**i frutti di mare** *ee froot·tee dee mah·reh*
spicy foods	**i cibi piccanti** *ee chee·bee peek·kahn·tee*
wheat	**il grano** *eel grah·noh*
Is it kosher?	**È kosher?** *eh koh·shehr*
Do you have...?	**Avete...?** *Ah·veh·teh*
skimmed milk	**latte scremato** *laht·teh skreh·mah·toh*
whole milk	**latte intero** *laht·teh een·teh·roh*
soya milk	**latte di soia** *laht·teh dee soh·jah*

Dining with Children

Do you have children's portions?	**Ci sono porzioni per bambini?** *chee soh·noh pohr·tsyoh·nee pehr bahm·bee·nee*
Can I have a highchair/child's seat?	**Un seggiolone/seggiolino da bambino, per favore.** *oon seh·djoh·loh·neh/seh·djoh·lee·noh dah bahm·bee·noh pehr fah·voh·reh*
Where can I feed/ change the baby?	**Dove posso dare da mangiare al/cambiare il bambino?** *doh·veh pohs·soh dah·reh dah mahn·jyah·reh ahl/kahm·byah·reh eel bahm·bee·noh*
Can you warm this?	**Me lo può scaldare?** *meh loh pwoh skahl·dah·reh*

For Traveling with Children, see page 143.

How to Complain

When will our food be ready?	**C'è ancora molto da aspettare?** *cheh ahn·koh·rah mohl·toh dah ah·speht·tah·reh*
We can't wait any longer.	**Non possiamo più aspettare.** *nohn pohs·syah·moh pyoo ah·speht·tah·reh*
We're leaving.	**Ce ne andiamo.** *cheh neh ahn·dyah·moh*
I didn't order this.	**Non è quello che ho ordinato.** *nohn eh kwehl·loh keh oh ohr·dee·nah·toh*

I ordered...	**Ho ordinato...** *oh ohr·dee·<u>nah</u>·toh...*
I can't eat this.	**Non lo posso mangiare.** *nohn loh <u>pohs</u>·soh mahn·<u>jyah</u>·reh*
This is too...	**È troppo...** *eh <u>trohp</u>·poh...*
cold/hot	**freddo/caldo** *<u>frehd</u>·doh/<u>kahl</u>·doh*
salty/spicy	**salato/piccante** *sah·<u>lah</u>·toh/peek·<u>kahn</u>·teh*
tough/bland	**duro/insipido** *<u>doo</u>·roh/een·<u>see</u>·pee·doh*
This isn't clean/fresh.	**Non è pulito/fresco.** *nohn eh poo·<u>lee</u>·toh/ <u>freh</u>·skoh*

Paying

The check [bill], please.	**Il conto, per favore.** *eel <u>kohn</u>·toh pehr fah·<u>voh</u>·reh*
Separate checks [bills], please.	**Conti separati, per favore.** *<u>kohn</u>·tee seh·pah·<u>rah</u>·tee pehr fah·<u>voh</u>·reh*
It's all together.	**Conto unico.** *<u>kohn</u>·toh <u>oo</u>·nee·koh*
Is service included?	**Il servizio è compreso?** *eel sehr·<u>vee</u>·tsyoh eh kohm·<u>preh</u>·zoh*
What's this amount for?	**Per cos'è questo importo?** *pehr koh·<u>zeh</u> <u>kweh</u>·stoh eem·<u>pohr</u>·toh*
I didn't have that. I had...	**Questo non è mio. Io ho mangiato...** *<u>kweh</u>·stoh nohn eh <u>mee</u>·oh ee·oh oh mahn·<u>jyah</u>·toh...*
Can I have a receipt/ an itemized bill?	**Posso avere la fattura/il conto dettagliato?** *<u>pohs</u>·soh ah·<u>veh</u>·reh lah faht·<u>too</u>·rah/ eel <u>kohn</u>·toh deht·tah·<u>llyah</u>·toh*
That was delicious!	**Era squisito!** *<u>eh</u>·rah skwee·<u>zee</u>·toh*
I've already paid	**L'ho gia pagato** *loh jyah pah·<u>gah</u>·toh*

Restaurants charge a **coperto** (service charge) but tipping 10–15% of the bill is common for good service. Tipping is customary in finer restaurants.

Meals & Cooking

Breakfast

l'acqua *lah·kwah*	water
gli affettati *llyee ahf·feht·tah·tee*	cold cuts [charcuterie]
il burro *eel boor·roh*	butter
il caffè/tè... *eel kahf·feh/teh...*	coffee/tea...
con il dolcificante *kohn eel dohl·chee·fee·kahn·teh*	with artificial sweetener
al latte *ahl laht·teh*	with milk
con lo zucchero *kohn loh dzook·keh·roh*	with sugar
decaffeinato *deh·kahf·feh·ee·nah·toh*	decaf
nero *neh·roh*	black
i cereali *ee cheh·reh·ah·lee*	cereal
la farina d'avena *lah fah·ree·nah dah·veh·nah*	oatmeal
il formaggio *eel fohr·mah·djoh*	cheese
la frittata *lah freet·tah·tah*	omelet
il latte *eel laht·teh*	milk
la marmellata *lah mahr·mehl·lah·tah*	jam
il muesli *eel mweh·slee*	granola [muesli]
il muffin *eel mahf·feen*	muffin
la pancetta *lah pahn·cheht·tah*	bacon
il pane *eel pah·neh*	bread
il pane tostato *eel pah·neh toh·stah·toh*	toast
il panino *eel pah·nee·noh*	roll
la salsiccia *lah sahl·see·chyah*	sausage
il succo... *eel sook·koh...*	...juice
d'arancia *dah·rahn·chyah*	orange
di mela *dee meh·lah*	apple
di pompelmo *dee pohm·pehl·moh*	grapefruit

l'uovo... _lwoh_·voh...	...egg
fritto _freet_·toh	fried
sodo/alla coque _soh_·doh/ahl·lah _kohk_	hard-/soft-boiled
strapazzato strah·pah·_tsah_·toh	scrambled
lo yogurt loh _yoh_·goort	yogurt

Appetizers

l'acciuga lah·_chyoo_·ghah	anchovy
l'affettato lahf·feht·tah·toh	platter of cold cuts
le alici a scapece leh ah·_lee_·chee ah skah·_peh_·cheh	fresh fried anchovies marinated in vinegar and spices
l'antipasto misto lahn·tee·_pah_·stoh _mee_·stoh	assorted appetizers
la bresaola lah breh·_sah_·oh·lah	cured raw beef
i carciofini sott'olio ee kar·chyoh·_fee_·nee soht·_toh_·lyoh	artichoke hearts in olive oil
la coppa lah _kohp_·pah	cured pork shoulder
i crostini ee kroh·_stee_·nee	toast topped with a variety of ingredients, including tomatoes, sardines and cheese
la caprese _lah_ kah·_preh_·seh	sliced tomatoes, mozzarella and basil dressed with olive oil
l'insalata di frutti di mare leen·sah·_lah_·tah dee _froot_·tee dee _mah_·reh	seafood salad
la mortadella lah mohr·tah·_dehl_·lah	Bologna sausage
la peperonata lah peh·peh·roh·_nah_·tah	mixed sweet peppers stewed with tomatoes
il prosciutto crudo di Parma eel proh·_shyoot_·toh _kroo_·doh dee _pahr_·mah	cured ham from Parma
i sottaceti ee soht·tah·_cheh_·tee	pickled vegetables

Soup

l'acquacotta *lah·kwah·koht·tah* — Tuscan vegetable soup with poached egg

il brodo di manzo *eel broh·doh dee mahn·dzoh* — beef broth

il brodo di pollo *eel broh·doh dee pohl·loh* — chicken broth

la buridda *lah boo·reed·dah* — fish stew

il cacciucco *eel kah·chyook·koh* — spicy seafood chowder

il cacciucco alla livornese *eel kah·chyook·koh ahl·lah lee·vohr·neh·seh* — tomato seafood chowder

la crema di legumi *lah kreh·mah dee leh·goo·mee* — vegetable cream soup

il minestrone *eel mee·neh·stroh·neh* — mixed vegetable and bean soup

la ribollita *lah ree·bohl·lee·tah* — Tuscan bean, vegetable and bread soup

lo spezzatino *loh speh·tsah·tee·noh* — meat stew

la zuppa di fagioli *lah dzoop·pah dee fah·jyoh·lee* — bean soup

la zuppa alla pavese *lah dzoop·pah ahl·lah pah·veh·seh* — consommé with poached egg, croutons and grated cheese

la zuppa di pollo *lah dzoop·pah dee pohl·loh* — chicken soup

la zuppa di pomodoro *lah dzoop·pah dee poh·moh·doh·roh* — tomato soup

la zuppa di verdure *lah dzoop·pah dee vehr·doo·reh* — vegetable soup

la zuppa di vongole *lah dzoop·pah dee vohn·goh·leh* — clam and white wine soup

Fish & Seafood

l'acciuga *lah·chyoo·ghah*	anchovy
l'anguilla *lahn·gweel·lah*	eel
l'anguilla alla veneziana *lahn·gweel·lah ahl·lah veh·neh·tsyah·nah*	eel cooked in tomato sauce, a specialty of Venice
l'aragosta *lah·rah·goh·stah*	lobster
l'aringa *lah·reen·gah*	herring
il baccalà *eel bahk·kah·lah*	salted, dried cod
il branzino *eel brahn·dzee·noh*	sea bass
i calamari *ee kah·lah·mah·ree*	squid
le cozze *leh koh·tseh*	mussels
le cozze ripiene *leh koh·tseh ree·pyeh·neh*	stuffed mussels
il fritto misto *eel freet·toh mee·stoh*	mixed fried fish with shellfish
i gamberi *ee gahm·beh·ree*	shrimp
i gamberi grigliati *ee gahm·beh·ree gree·llyah·tee*	grilled shrimp with garlic
il granchio *eel grahn·kyoh*	crab
le lumache *leh loo·mah·keh*	snails
le lumache alla milanese *leh loo·mah·keh ahl·lah mee·lah·neh·seh*	snails with anchovy, fennel and wine sauce
il merluzzo *eel mehr·loo·tsoh*	cod
la moleca *lah moh·leh·kah*	soft shell crab
l'orata *loh·rah·tah*	sea bream
le ostriche *leh oh·stree·keh*	oysters
il pesce spada *eel peh·sheh spah·dah*	swordfish
il polpo *eel pohl·poh*	octopus
il salmone *eel sahl·moh·neh*	salmon
la sardina *lah sahr·dee·nah*	sardine
lo scorfano *loh skohr·fah·noh*	hog fish
la sogliola *lah soh·llyoh·lah*	sole

lo stoccafisso *loh stohk·kah·<u>fees</u>·soh* — dried cod cooked with tomatoes, olives and artichoke

il tonno *eel <u>tohn</u>·noh* — tuna

la trota *lah <u>troh</u>·tah* — trout

le vongole *leh <u>vohn</u>·goh·leh* — clams

Meat & Poultry

l'abbacchio alla romana *lahb·<u>bahk</u>·kyoh <u>ahl</u>·lah roh·<u>mah</u>·nah* — roasted spring lamb, a specialty of Rome

l'agnello *lah·<u>nyehl</u>·loh* — lamb

l'anatra *<u>lah</u>·nah·trah* — duck

la bistecca *lah bee·<u>stehk</u>·kah* — steak

la bistecca alla fiorentina *lah bee·<u>stehk</u>·kah <u>ahl</u>·lah fyoh·rehn·<u>tee</u>·nah* — grilled T-bone steak, a specialty of Florence

la braciola *lah brah·<u>chyoh</u>·lah* — grilled pork chop

il capretto *eel kah·<u>preht</u>·toh* — goat

la cima alla genovese *lah <u>chee</u>·mah <u>ahl</u>·lah jeh·noh·<u>veh</u>·seh* — flank steak stuffed with eggs and vegetables, a specialty of Genoa

il cinghiale *eel cheen·<u>ghyah</u>·leh* — wild boar, usually braised or roasted

il coniglio *eel koh·<u>nee</u>·llyoh* — rabbit

la cotoletta alla milanese *lah koh·toh·<u>leht</u>·tah <u>ahl</u>·lah mee·lah·<u>neh</u>·seh* — breaded veal cutlet flavored with cheese

la cotoletta di vitello con fontina *lah koh·toh·<u>leht</u>·tah dee vee·<u>tehl</u>·loh kohn fohn·<u>tee</u>·nah* — veal cutlet stuffed with fontina cheese, breaded and sautéed

il fagiano *eel fah·<u>jyah</u>·noh* — pheasant

il fegato *eel <u>feh</u>·gah·toh* — liver

il fegato alla veneziana *eel <u>feh</u>·gah·toh <u>ahl</u>·lah veh·neh·<u>tsyah</u>·nah* — thin slices of calf's liver fried with onions

il filetto al pepe verde *eel fee-leht-toh ahl peh-peh vehr-deh*
filet steak in a creamy sauce with green peppercorns

gli involtini *llyee een-vohl-tee-nee*
thin slices of meat rolled and stuffed

la luganega *lah loo-gah-neh-gah*
type of pork sausage

il maiale *eel mah-yah-leh*
pork

il manzo *eel mahn-dzoh*
beef

il montone *eel mohn-toh-neh*
mutton

l'oca *loh-kah*
goose

l'osso buco *lohs-soh boo-koh*
braised veal shank

la pancetta *lah pahn-cheht-tah*
bacon

la piccata al Marsala *lah peek-kah-tah ahl mahr-sah-lah*
thin cutlets cooked in Marsala sauce

il pollo *eel pohl-loh*
chicken

il pollo alla cacciatora *eel pohl-loh ahl-lah kah-chyah-toh-rah*
chicken braised with mushrooms in tomato sauce

il pollo alla diavola *eel pohl-loh ahl-lah dyah-voh-lah*
chicken grilled with lemon and hot pepper

il pollo al mattone *eel pohl-loh ahl maht-toh-neh*
chicken cooked with herbs in a brick oven

il pollo alla romana *eel pohl-loh ahl-lah roh-mah-nah*
diced chicken with tomato sauce and sweet peppers

la polpetta *lah pohl-peht-tah*
meatball

la porchetta *lah pohr-keht-tah*
suckling pig

il prosciutto *eel proh-shyoot-toh*
ham

la quaglia *lah kwah-llyah*
quail

la salsiccia *lah sahl-see-chyah*
sausage

il saltimbocca *eel sahl-teem-bohk-kah*
veal and ham roll

il tacchino *eel tahk-kee-noh*
turkey

il vitello *eel vee-tehl-loh*
veal

Vegetables & Staples

l'aceto *lah·cheh·toh* — vinegar
l'aglio *lah·llyoh* — garlic
l'asparago *lah·spah·rah·goh* — asparagus
l'avocado *lah·voh·kah·doh* — avocado
la barbabietola *lah bahr·bah·byeh·toh·lah* — beet
la bietola *lah byeh·toh·lah* — swiss chard
i broccoli *ee brohk·koh·lee* — broccoli
il carciofo *eel kahr·chyoh·foh* — artichoke
i carciofi alla guidea *ee kahr·chyoh·fee ahl·lah gwee·deh·ah* — crispy deep-fried artichokes, originally a specialty of the Jewish quarter in Rome

i carciofi alla romana *ee kahr·chyoh·fee ahl·lah roh·mah·nah* — whole lightly stewed artichokes stuffed with garlic, salt, olive oil, wild mint and parsley

la carota *lah kah·roh·tah* — carrot
il cavolfiore *eel kah·vohl·fyoh·reh* — cauliflower
il cavolo *eel kah·voh·loh* — cabbage
i ceci *ee cheh·chee* — chickpeas
il cetriolo *eel cheh·tryoh·loh* — cucumber
la cipolla *lah chee·pohl·lah* — onion
i fagioli *ee fah·jyoh·lee* — beans
i fagioli alla toscana *ee fah·jyoh·lee ahl·lah toh·skah·nah* — Tuscan-style beans seasoned with salt, black pepper and olive oil

i fagioli in umido *ee fah·jyoh·lee een oo·mee·doh* — beans cooked in tomato sauce and spices
i fagiolini *ee fah·jyoh·lee·nee* — green beans
le fave *leh fah·veh* — broad beans

i funghi *ee foon·ghee* mushrooms
i funghi porcini arrostiti *ee foon·ghee* porcini mushrooms
pohr·chee·nee ahr·roh·stee·tee roasted or grilled with garlic,
parsley and chili peppers

la lattuga *lah laht·too·gah* lettuce
il mais *eel mah·ees* corn
la melanzana *lah meh·lahn·tsah·nah* eggplant [aubergine]
l'oliva *loh·lee·vah* olive
l'ortaggio *lohr·tah·djoh* vegetable
la pasta *lah pah·stah* pasta
la patata *lah pah·tah·tah* potato
il pepe bianco/nero *eel peh·peh* white/black
byahn·koh/neh·roh pepper
il pepe rosso *eel peh·peh rohs·soh* paprika
il peperone rosso/verde red/green pepper
eel peh·peh·roh·neh rohs·soh/vehr·deh
i piselli *ee pee·tsehl·lee* peas
i piselli al prosciutto *ee pee·tsehl·lee ahl* peas with ham
proh·shyoot·toh
la polenta *lah poh·lehn·tah* cornmeal
la polenta al nero di seppia polenta with baby
lah poh·lehn·tah ahl neh·roh dee sehp·pyah squid in its own ink
il pomodoro *eel poh·moh·doh·roh* tomato
i porri con le patate *ee pohr·ree kohn* leek and potato
leh pah·tah·teh casserole
la pizza *lah pee·tsah* pizza
il riso *eel ree·zoh* rice
il risotto *eel ree·zoh·toh* arborio rice cooked slowly
in broth, with seafood,
vegetables, etc.

il sedano *eel seh·dah·noh* celery

gli spinaci *llyee spee·<u>nah</u>·chee* — spinach
lo zucchero *loh <u>tsook</u>·keh·roh* — sugar
la zucchina *lah tsook·<u>kee</u>·nah* — zucchini [courgette]

In Italy, pizza is generally served in a size suitable for one person, though it can be shared. Pizza is usually thin crusted, about the size of a dinner plate, and is eaten with a knife and fork. Some pizzerias, though, may ask if you want your pizza **sottile** (thin) or **alta** (literally, high; here it means thick). There are many varieties of pizza and most are topped with mozzarella cheese; listed in the menu reader are some of the most popular.

Fruit

l'ananas *lah·nah·nahs* — pineapple
l'anguria *lahn·<u>goo</u>·ryah* — watermelon (northern Italy)
l'albicocca *lahl·bee·<u>kohk</u>·kah* — apricot
l'arancia *lah·<u>rahn</u>·chah* — orange
la banana *lah bah·<u>nah</u>·nah* — banana
il cedro *eel <u>cheh</u>·droh* — lime
la ciliegia *lah chee·<u>lyeh</u>·jyah* — cherry
il cocomero *eel koh·<u>koh</u>·meh·roh* — watermelon (Rome & southern Italy)

la fragola *lah <u>frah</u>·goh·lah* — strawberry
la frutta *lah <u>froot</u>·tah* — fruit
il lampone *eel lahm·<u>poh</u>·neh* — raspberry
il limone *eel lee·<u>moh</u>·neh* — lemon
la mela *lah <u>meh</u>·lah* — apple
il melone *eel meh·<u>loh</u>·neh* — melon

il mirtillo *eel meer·teel·loh*   blueberry
la pera *lah peh·rah*   pear
la pesca *lah peh·skah*   peach
il pompelmo *eel pohm·pehl·moh*   grapefruit
la prugna *lah proo·nyah*   plum
l'uva *loo·vah*   grape

Cheese

il formaggio… *eel fohr·mah·djoh…*   …cheese
  asiago *ah·syah·goh*   nutty-flavored
  Bel Paese *behl pah·eh·seh*   smooth and delicate
  bocconcini *bohk·kohn·chee·nee*   small balls of fresh mozzarella
  caciocavallo *kah·chyoh·kah·vahl·loh*   firm, slightly sweet, made
    with cow's or sheep's milk
  caciotta *kah·chyoht·tah*   firm, usually mild
  caprino *kah·pree·noh*   made from goat's milk
  crescenza *kreh·shehn·tsah*   rich and creamy
  dolce *dohl·cheh*   mild
  dolcelatte *dohl·cheh·laht·teh*   mild, creamy, blue-veined
  duro *doo·roh*   hard
  fontina *fohn·tee·nah*   full-fat and semi-hard

gorgonzola *gohr·gohn·dzoh·lah* strong and blue-veined
grana *grah·nah* similar to parmesan
gruviera *groo·vyeh·rah* sweet, nutlike flavor,
similar to Swiss gruyere

mascarpone *mahs·kahr·poh·neh* used like whipped cream
molle *mohl·leh* soft
mozzarella *moh·tsah·rehl·lah* full-fat and mild, made with
cow's or buffalo's milk

parmigiano *pahr·mee·jyah·noh* parmesan
pecorino *peh·koh·ree·noh* strong, made with
sheep's milk

piccante *peek·kahn·teh* sharp
provolone *proh·voh·loh·neh* firm and flavorful
ricotta *ree·koht·tah* soft and mild, made with
cow's or sheep's milk

Dessert

gli amaretti *llyee ah·mah·reht·tee* almond cookies
il biscotto *eel bees·koht·toh* crunchy cookie for dipping
into coffee or wine

il budino *eel boo·dee·noh* pudding
i cannoli *ee kahn·noh·lee* crispy pastry tubes filled
with sweetened ricotta and
candied fruit

la cassata siciliana *lah kahs·sah·tah* traditional Sicilian cake with
see·chee·lyah·nah ricotta, chocolate and
candied fruit

il castagnaccio *eel kah·stah·nyah·chyoh* deep-fried chestnut cake
la crema *lah kreh·mah* custard
la crostata *lah kroh·stah·tah* pie
i dolci *ee dohl·chee* sweets

il gelato *eel jeh-lah-toh*	ice cream
i gianduiotti *ee jyahn-dyoht-tee*	chocolate drops from Turin
la granita *lah grah-nee-tah*	frozen fruit-juice slush
il pandolce *eel pahn-dohl-cheh*	yeast cake with grapes and raisins
il panettone *eel pah-neht-toh-neh*	Christmas sweet bread with raisins and candied citrus peel
il panforte *eel pahn-fohr-teh*	dense cake made of almond, candied citrus, spices and honey
la panna cotta *lah pahn-nah koht-tah*	molded chilled cream pudding
il tartufo *eel tahr-too-foh*	chocolate truffle dessert
il tiramisù *eel tee-rah-mee-soo*	coffee- and rum-flavored layered dessert
la torta *lah tohr-tah*	cake
lo zabaglione *loh dzah-bah-llyoh-neh*	warm custard with Marsala wine
lo zuccotto *loh dzook-koht-toh*	sponge cake filled with fresh cream, chocolate, candied fruit and liqueur

The Italian **gelato**, similar to ice cream, is made from milk and sugar—not cream. Though it has less fat content than ice cream, it is still very dense and creamy. Popular flavors include **caffè** (coffee), **cioccolato** (chocolate), **fragola** (strawberry), **frutti di bosco** (mixed berries), **gianduia** (chocolate hazelnut), **limone** (lemon), **nocciola** (hazelnut), **pistacchio** (pistachio) and **vaniglia** (vanilla).

Sauces & Condiments

salt	**sale** *sah·leh*
pepper	**pepe** *peh·peh*
mustard	**senape** *seh·nah·peh*
ketchup	**ketchup** *keh·chyahp*

At the Market

Where are the carts [trolleys]/baskets?	**Dove sono i carrelli/cestini?** *doh·veh soh·noh ee kahr·rehl·lee/cheh·stee·nee*
Where is/ Where are…?	**Dov'è/Dove sono…?** *doh·veh/doh·veh soh·noh…*
I'd like some of that/this.	**Vorrei un po' di quello/questo.** *vohr·ray oon poh dee kwehl·loh/kweh·stoh*
Can I taste it?	**Posso assaggiarlo?** *pohs·soh ahs·sah·djahr·loh*
I'd like…	**Vorrei…** *vohr·ray…*
a kilo/half-kilo of…	**un chilo/mezzo chilo di…** *oon kee·loh/meh·dzoh kee·loh dee…*
a liter of…	**un litro di…** *oon lee·troh dee…*
a piece of…	**un pezzo di…** *oon peh·tsoh dee…*
a slice of…	**una fetta di…** *oo·nah feht·tah dee…*
More/Less.	**Di più/Di meno.** *dee pyoo/dee meh·noh*
How much?	**Quant'è?** *kwahn·teh*

Where do I pay?	**Dove si paga?** <u>doh</u>•veh see <u>pah</u>•gah
A bag, please.	**Una busta, per favore.** <u>oo</u>•nah <u>boos</u>•tah pehr fah•<u>voh</u>•reh
I'm being helped.	**Mi stanno servendo.** mee <u>stahn</u>•noh sehr•<u>vehn</u>•doh

Visit a **panetteria** (bakery) for fresh and tasty bread products; a **gastronomia** (delicatessen) for cold cuts, prepared meals sold by weight and fresh sandwiches; a **pasticceria** (pastry shop) for desserts; a **gelateria** (ice cream parlor) for ice cream specialties or a **bar** or **caffè** (cafe) for a variety of refreshments and small meals, which are cheaper if consumed standing, but more expensive for table service. You can find inexpensive food items at a local **supermercato** (supermarket).

YOU MAY HEAR...

Posso aiutarla? <u>pohs</u>•soh ah•yoo•<u>tahr</u>•lah	Can I help you?
Desidera? deh•<u>zee</u>•deh•rah	What would you like?
Altro? <u>ahl</u>•troh	Anything else?
Sono...euro. <u>soh</u>•noh...<u>eh</u>•oo•roh	That's...euros.

In the Kitchen

blender	**il frullatore** eel frool•lah•<u>toh</u>•reh
bottle opener	**l'apribottiglie** lah•pree•boht•<u>tee</u>•llyeh
bowl	**la coppa** lah <u>kohp</u>•pah
can opener	**l'apriscatole** lah•pree•<u>skah</u>•toh•leh

chopsticks	**i bastoncini cinesi** *ee bah•stohn•<u>chee</u>•nee <u>chee</u>•neh•see*
colander	**lo scolapasta** *lah skoh•lah•<u>pah</u>•stah*
corkscrew	**il cavatappi** *eel kah•vah•<u>tahp</u>•pee*
cup	**la tazza** *lah <u>tah</u>•tsah*
fork	**la forchetta** *lah fohr•<u>keht</u>•tah*
frying pan	**la padella** *lah pah•<u>dehl</u>•lah*
glass	**il bicchiere** *eel beek•<u>kyeh</u>•reh*
knife	**il coltello** *eel kohl•<u>tehl</u>•loh*
measuring cup/ spoon	**la tazza di misurazione/il misurino** *lah <u>tah</u>•tsah dee mee•soo•rah•<u>tsyoh</u>•neh/eel mee•soo•<u>ree</u>•noh*
napkin	**il tovagliolo** *eel toh•vah•<u>llyoh</u>•loh*
plate	**il piatto** *eel <u>pyaht</u>•toh*
pot	**la pentola** *lah <u>pehn</u>•toh•lah*
spatula	**la spatola** *lah <u>spah</u>•toh•lah*
spoon	**il cucchiaio** *eel kook•<u>kyah</u>•yoh*

Measurements in Europe are metric - and that applies to the weight of food too. If you tend to think in pounds and ounces, it's worth brushing up on what the metric equivalent is before you go shopping for fruit and veg in markets and supermarkets. Five hundred grams, or half a kilo, is a common quantity to order, and that converts to just over a pound (17.65 ounces, to be precise).

YOU MAY SEE...

CALORIE	calories
SENZA GRASSI	fat free
CONSERVARE IN FRIGO	keep refrigerated
PUÒ CONTENERE TRACCE DI...	may contain traces of...
PUÒ ESSERE COTTO AL MICROONDE	microwaveable
DA CONSUMARE PREFERIBILMENTE ENTRO...	sell by...
ADATTO AI VEGETARIANI	suitable for vegetarians

Drinks

ESSENTIAL

Can I have the wine/ drink menu, please?	**La carta dei vini/lista delle bevande, per favore.** *lah kahr·tah day vee·nee/lee·stah dehl·leh beh·vahn·deh pehr fah·voh·reh*
What do you recommend?	**Cosa mi consiglia?** *koh·zah mee kohn·see·llyah*
I'd like a bottle/ glass of red/ white wine.	**Vorrei una bottiglia/un bicchiere di vino rosso/bianco.** *vohr·ray oo·nah boht·tee·llyah/ oon beek·kyeh·reh dee vee·noh rohs·soh/byahn·koh*
The house wine, please.	**Il vino della casa, per favore.** *eel vee·noh dehl·lah kah·zah pehr fah·voh·reh*
Another bottle/ glass, please.	**Un'altra bottiglia/Un altro bicchiere, per favore.** *oo·nahl·trah boht·tee·llyah/oo·nahl·troh beek·kyeh·reh pehr fah·voh·reh*
I'd like a local beer.	**Vorrei una birra locale.** *vohr·ray oo·nah beer·rah loh·kah·leh*
Cheers!	**Salute!** *sah·loo·teh*

Can I buy you a drink?	**Posso offrirle qualcosa?** _pohs·soh_
	ohf·**freer**·leh kwahl·**koh**·sah
A coffee/tea, please.	**Un caffè/tè, per favore.** _oon kahf·**feh**/teh pehr fah·**voh**·reh_
Black.	**Nero.** _neh·roh_
With...	**Con...** _kohn..._
some milk	**un po' di latte** _oon poh dee **laht**·teh_
sugar	**lo zucchero** _loh **dzook**·keh·roh_
artificial sweetener	**il dolcificante** _eel dohl·chee·fee·**kahn**·teh_
..., please.	**..., per favore.** _...pehr fah·**voh**·reh_
A juice	**Un succo** _oon **sook**·koh_
A soda	**Una bibita** _**oo**·nah **bee**·bee·tah_
A (sparkling/still) water	**Un bicchiere d'acqua (frizzante/naturale)** _oon beek·**kyeh**·reh **dah**·kwah (free·**dzahn**·teh/ nah·too·**rah**·leh)_

Non-alcoholic Drinks

l'acqua (frizzante/naturale) _**lah**·kwah (free·**dzahn**·teh/nah·too·**rah**·leh)_	water (sparkling/still)
la bibita _lah **bee**·bee·tah_	soda
il caffè _eel kahf·**feh**_	coffee
il latte _eel **laht**·teh_	milk
la limonata _lah lee·moh·**nah**·tah_	lemon soda
il succo _eel **sook**·koh_	juice
il tè (freddo) _eel teh (**frehd**·doh)_	(iced) tea
la spremuta _lah spreh·**moo**·tah_	fresh-squeezed fruit juice

Il caffè (coffee) has been a very popular drink in Italy since the 16th century, when the first European coffeehouse opened in Venice. Italians usually stop to drink a coffee—standing at the bar—on their way to work. If you have time to spare, you may wish to sit and enjoy your beverage, but you'll pay extra for table service. It is customary to have a cup of coffee after your meal. Popular types of Italian coffee include:

caffè: strong coffee, similar to espresso elsewhere
doppio: double serving of **caffè**
ristretto: very strong coffee, made with less water
americano: weak coffee, made with more water
macchiato: coffee served with steamed milk
cappuccino: equal parts coffee, steamed milk and milk foam

Aperitifs, Cocktails & Liqueurs

l'amaretto lah·mah·_reht_·toh	almond liqueur
l'amaro lah·_mah_·roh	bitter
il brandy eel _brahn_·dee	brandy
il digestivo eel dee·jehs·_tee_·voh	after-dinner drink

il gin *eel jeen*   gin
il rum *eel room*   rum
la sambuca *lah sahm·boo·kah*   aniseed-flavored liqueur
lo scotch *loh skohtch*   scotch
la strega *lah streh·gah*   sweet herb liqueur
la tequila *la teh·kee·lah*   tequila
la vodka *la vohd·kah*   vodka
il whisky *eel whees·kee*   whisky

YOU MAY HEAR...

Posso offrirle qualcosa?   Can I get you a drink?
pohs·soh ohf·freer·leh kwahl·koh·zah

Con latte o zucchero?   With milk or sugar?
kohn laht·teh oh dzook·keh·roh

Acqua frizzante o naturale? *ah·kwah*   Sparkling or still water?
free·dzahn·teh oh nah·too·rah·leh

Beer

la birra... *lah beer·rah...*   ...beer
  in bottiglia/alla spina   bottled/draft
  een boht·tee·llyah/ahl·lah spee·nah

  scura/chiara *skoo·rah/kyah·rah*   dark/light
  lager/pilsner *lah·gehr/peels·nehr*   lager/pilsner
  nazionale/importata   local/imported
  nah·tsyoh·nah·leh/eem·pohr·tah·tah

  analcolica *ah·nahl·koh·lee·kah*   non-alcoholic

Wine

lo champagne *loh shahm·pah·nyeh*   champagne
il vino... *eel vee·noh...*   ...wine
   rosso/bianco *rohs·soh/byahn·koh*   red/white
   della casa/da tavola *dehl·lah*   house/table
   kah·zah/dah tah·voh·lah
   secco/dolce *sehk·koh/dohl·cheh*   dry/sweet
   frizzante *free·dzahn·teh*   sparkling
   da dessert *dah dehs·sehrt*   dessert

Popular types of Italian wine are listed below. The region where
the wine is typically found is listed in parentheses.

sparkling sweet wine	Asti spumante (Piedmont); Prosecco (Veneto)
red wine	Nebbiolo (Piedmont); Amarone, Valpolicella (Veneto); Brunello di Montalcino, Chianti, Sangiovese (Tuscany); Corvo Rosso, Nero d'Avola (Sicily)
rosé	Lagrein (Trentino-Alto Adige)
dry white wine	Frascati (Latium); Orvieto (Umbria); Pinot grigio (Veneto); Vermentino (Sardinia)
dessert wine	Vin santo (Tuscany)

On the Menu

l'abbacchio *lahb·bahk·kyoh* — lamb

l'acciuga *lah·chyoo·ghah* — anchovy

l'aceto *lah·cheh·toh* — vinegar

l'aceto balsamico *lah·cheh·toh bahl·sah·mee·koh* — balsamic vinegar

l'acqua *lah·kwah* — water

l'acqua tonica *lah·kwah toh·nee·kah* — tonic water

gli affettati *llyee ahf·feht·tah·tee* — cold cuts [charcuterie]

l'agliata *lah·llyah·tah* — garlic sauce

l'aglio *lah·llyoh* — garlic

l'agnello *lah·nyehl·loh* — lamb

l'albicocca *lahl·bee·kohk·kah* — apricot

l'albume *lahl·boo·meh* — egg white

gli alcolici *llyee ahl·koh·lee·chee* — spirits

l'alloro *lahl·loh·roh* — bay leaf

l'amarena *lah·mah·reh·nah* — sour cherry

l'ananas *lah·nah·nahs* — pineapple

l'anatra *lah·nah·trah* — duck

l'aneto *lah·neh·toh* — dill

l'anguilla *lahn·gweel·lah* — eel

l'anguria *lahn·goo·ryah* — watermelon (northern Italy)

l'aperitivo *lah·peh·ree·tee·voh* — aperitif

l'arachide *lah·rah·kee·deh* — peanut

l'aragosta *lah·rah·goh·stah* — lobster

l'arancia *lah·rahn·chyah* — orange

l'aringa *lah·reen·gah* — herring

l'arrosto *lahr·roh·stoh* — roast

gli aromi *llyee ah·roh·mee* — herbs

l'asparago *lah·spah·rah·goh* — asparagus

l'avocado *lah·voh·kah·doh*	avocado
il baccalà *eel bahk·kah·lah*	salted, dried cod
la banana *lah bah·nah·nah*	banana
la barbabietola *lah bahr·bah·byeh·toh·lah*	beet
il basilico *eel bah·see·lee·koh*	basil
la bibita *lah bee·bee·tah*	soda
la bietola *lah byeh·toh·lah*	swiss chard
la birra *lah beer·rah*	beer
il biscotto *eel bee·skoht·toh*	cookie [biscuit]
la bistecca *lah bee·stehk·kah*	steak
la braciola *lah brah·chyoh·lah*	grilled pork chop
il brandy *eel brahn·dee*	brandy
il branzino *eel brahn·dzee·noh*	sea bass
i broccoli *ee brohk·koh·lee*	broccoli
il brodo *eel broh·doh*	broth
il budino *eel boo·dee·noh*	pudding
il bue *eel boo·eh*	ox
la burrida *lah boo·reed·dah*	fish stew (Genova)
il burro *eel boor·roh*	butter
il caffè *eel kahf·feh*	coffee
i calamari *ee kah·lah·mah·ree*	squid
la cannella *lah kahn·nehl·lah*	cinnamon
il cappero *eel kahp·peh·roh*	caper
la capra *lah kah·prah*	goat
il capretto *eel kah·preht·toh*	kid (baby goat)
le caramelle *leh kah·rah·mehl·leh*	candy [sweets]
il caramello *eel kah·rah·mehl·loh*	caramel
il carciofo *eel kahr·chyoh·foh*	artichoke
i cardi *ee kahr·dee*	cardoons (relative of the artichoke)
la carne *lah kahr·neh*	meat

la carne in scatola *lah kahr•neh een skah•toh•lah* — corned beef

la carne tritata *lah kahr•neh tree•tah•tah* — ground meat

la carota *lah kah•roh•tah* — carrot

la castagna *lah kah•stah•nyah* — chestnut

il cavolfiore *eel kah•vohl•fyoh•reh* — cauliflower

i cavoletti di Bruxelles *ee kah•voh•leht•tee dee broo•ksehl* — Brussels sprouts

il cavolo *eel kah•voh•loh* — cabbage

il cavolo rosso *eel kah•voh•loh rohs•soh* — red cabbage

i ceci *ee cheh•chee* — chickpeas

il cedro *eel cheh•droh* — lime

i cereali *ee cheh•reh•ah•lee* — cereal

il cervo *eel chehr•voh* — venison

il cetriolino *eel cheh•tryoh•lee•noh* — gherkin

il cetriolo *eel cheh•tryoh•loh* — cucumber

la ciambella fritta *lah chahm•behl•lah freet•tah* — doughnut

il chiodo di garofano *eel kyoh•doh dee gah•roh•fah•noh* — clove

la cicoria *lah chee•koh•ryah* — chicory

la ciliegia *lah chee•lyeh•jyah* — cherry

il cinghiale *eel cheen•ghyah•leh* — wild boar

il cioccolato *eel chyohk•koh•lah•toh* — chocolate

la cipolla *lah chee•pohl•lah* — onion

la cipollina verde *lah chee•pohl•lee•nah vehr•deh* — scallion [spring onion]

il cocco *eel kohk•koh* — coconut

il cocomero *eel koh•koh•meh•roh* — watermelon (Rome and southern Italy)

la coda di bue *lah koh•dah dee boo•eh* — oxtail

la confettura *lah kohn•feht•too•rah*	jam
il coniglio *eel koh•nee•llyoh*	rabbit
la conserva *lah kohn•sehr•vah*	tomato paste
il consommé *eel kohn•sohm•meh*	consommé
la coppa *lah kohp•pah*	cured pork shoulder
il cornetto *eel kohr•neht•toh*	croissant
la coscia *lah koh•shah*	leg
le cozze *leh koh•tseh*	mussel
il cracker *eel krah•kehr*	cracker
i crauti *ee krawoo•tee*	sauerkraut
la crema *lah kreh•mah*	custard
il crescione *eel kreh•shyoh•neh*	watercress
le crespelle *leh kreh•spehl•leh*	crepes
la crostata *lah kroh•stah•tah*	pie
il cumino *eel koo•mee•noh*	caraway/cumin
i datteri *ee daht•teh•ree*	dates
il digestivo *eel dee•jeh•stee•voh*	after-dinner drink
il dolcificante *eel dohl•chee•fee•kahn•teh*	sweetener
il dragoncello *eel drah•gohn•chehl•loh*	tarragon
l'erba cipollina *lehr•bah chee•pohl•lee•nah*	chives
l'erbetta *lehr•beht•teh*	herb

l'espresso *leh·sprehs·soh* — coffee

il fagiano *eel fah·jyah·noh* — pheasant

il fagiolino *eel fah·jyoh·lee·noh* — green bean

i fagioli di soya *ee fah·jyoh·dee soh·yah* — soybean [soya bean]

il fagiolo *eel fah·jyoh·loh* — bean

la faraona *lah fah·rah·oh·nah* — guinea fowl

la farina *lah fah·ree·nah* — flour

la farina d'avena *lah fah·ree·nah dah·veh·nah* — oatmeal

la farina di mais *lah fah·ree·nah dee mah·ees* — cornmeal

il fegato *eel feh·gah·toh* — liver

il filetto *eel fee·leht·toh* — filet

il fico *eel fee·koh* — fig

il finocchio *eel fee·nohk·kyoh* — fennel

il formaggio *eel fohr·mah·djoh* — cheese

il formaggio caprino *eel fohr·mah·djoh kah·pree·noh* — goat cheese

il formaggio cremoso *eel fohr·mah·djoh kreh·moh·zoh* — cream cheese

i fiocchi di latte *ee fyohk·kee dee laht·teh* — cottage cheese

la fragola *lah frah·goh·lah* — strawberry

la frittata *lah freet·tah·tah* — omelet

la frittella *lah freet·tehl·lah* — fritter/pancake

il frullatto *eel frool·lah·toh* — milkshake

la frutta *lah froot·tah* — fruit

la frutta cotta *lah froot·tah koht·tah* — stewed fruit

i frutti di bosco *ee froot·tee dee boh·skoh* — mixed berries

i frutti di mare *ee froot·tee dee mah·reh* — seafood/shellfish

il fungo *eel foon·goh* — mushroom

la gallina *lah gahl·lee·nah* — hen

il gambero *eel gahm·beh·roh* — shrimp

la gelatina *lah jeh·lah·tee·nah* — jelly

il gelato *eel jeh·lah·toh* — ice cream

il germoglio di soia *eel jehr·moh·llyoh dee soh·yah* — bean sprouts

il ghiaccio *eel ghyah·chyoh* — ice (cube)

il gin *eel geen* — gin

il gorgonzola *eel gohr·gohn·dzoh·lah* — blue cheese

il granchio *eel grahn·kyoh* — crab

il grano *eel grah·noh* — wheat

la guava *lah gwah·vah* — guava

l'hamburger *lahm·boor·gehr* — hamburger

l'indivia *leen·dee·vyah* — endive

l'insalata *leen·sah·lah·tah* — salad

il ketchup *eel keht·choop* — ketchup

il kiwi *eel kee·wee* — kiwi

il lampone *eel lahm·poh·neh* — raspberry

il latte *eel laht·teh* — milk

il latte di soia *eel laht·teh dee soh·yah* — soymilk [soya milk]

la lattuga *lah laht·too·gah* — lettuce

la lenticchia *lah lehn·teek·kyah* — lentil

la limonata *lah lee·moh·nah·tah* — lemon soda

il limone *eel lee·moh·neh* — lemon

la lingua *lah leen·gwah* — tongue

il liquore *eel lee·kwoh·reh* — liqueur

il liquore all'arancia *eel lee·kwoh·reh ahl·lah·rahn·chyah* — orange liqueur

il lombo *eel lohm·boh* — loin/sirloin

la lumaca *lah loo·mah·kah* — snail

i maccheroni *ee mahk·keh·roh·nee* — macaroni

il maiale *eel mah·yah·leh* — pork

il maialino da latte *eel mah·yah·lee·noh dah laht·teh* — suckling pig

la maionese *lah mah·yoh·neh·zeh* — mayonnaise

il mais dolce *eel mah·ees dohl·cheh* — sweet corn

il mandarino *eel mahn·dah·ree·noh* — tangerine

la mandorla *lah mahn·dohr·lah* — almond

il mango *eel mahn·goh* — mango

il manzo *eel mahn·dzoh* — beef

la margarina *lah mahr·gah·ree·nah* — margarine

la marmellata *lah mahr·mehl·lah·tah* — marmalade/jam

il marzapane *eel mahr·dzah·pah·neh* — marzipan

la mela *lah meh·lah* — apple

la melanzana *lah meh·lahn·tsah·nah* — eggplant [aubergine]

il melograno *eel meh·loh·grah·noh* — pomegranate

il melone *eel meh·loh·neh* — melon

la menta *lah mehn·tah* — mint

la merenda *lah meh·rehn·dah* — snack

la meringa *lah meh·reen·gah* — meringue

il merluzzo *eel mehr·loo·tsoh* — cod

il miele *eel myeh·leh* — honey

il minestrone *eel mee·neh·stroh·neh* — vegetable and bean soup

il mirtillo *eel meer·teel·loh* — blueberry

il montone *eel mohn·toh·neh* — mutton

la mora *lah moh·rah* — blackberry

la mortadella *lah mohr·tah·dehl·lah* — Bologna sausage

il muesli *eel mweh·slee* — granola [muesli]

il muffin *eel mahf·feen* — muffin

il nasello *eel nah·zehl·loh* — hake

la nocciola *lah noh·chyoh·lah* — hazelnut

la noce *lah noh·cheh* — walnut

la noce moscata *lah noh·cheh moh·skah·tah* — nutmeg

la nutella *lah noo·tehl·lah* — hazelnut-flavored chocolate spread

l'oca *loh·kah* — goose

l'olio d'oliva *loh·lyoh doh·lee·vah* — olive oil

l'oliva *loh·lee·vah* — olive

l'orata *loh·rah·tah* — sea bream

l'origano *loh·ree·gah·noh* — oregano

l'ortaggio *lohr·tah·djoh* — vegetable

l'orzo *lohr·tsoh* — barley

l'ostrica *loh·stree·kah* — oyster

il palombo *eel pah·lohm·boh* — dogfish

la pancetta *lah pahn·cheht·tah* — bacon

il pane *eel pah·neh* — bread

il pane tostato *eel pah·neh toh·stah·toh* — toast

il panino *eel pah·nee·noh* — roll/sandwich

la panna acida *lah pahn·nah ah·chee·dah* — sour cream

la panna montata *lah pahn·nah mohn·tah·tah* — whipped cream

la papaya *lah pah·pah·yah* — papaya

la pasta *lah pah·stah* — pastry

pasta *pah·stah* — pasta

  gli agnolotti *llyee ah·nyoh·loht·tee* — meat-stuffed pasta

  i cannelloni *ee kahn·nehl·loh·nee* — stuffed pasta tubes, topped with sauce

  i cappelletti *ee kahp·pehl·leht·tee* — small ravioli filled with meat, ham, cheese and eggs

  i capelli d'angelo *ee kah·pehl·lee dahn·jeh·loh* — angelhair pasta

  le fettuccine *leh feht·too·chee·neh* — broad, long pasta made from eggs and flour

  i fusilli *ee foo·seel·lee* — spiral-shaped pasta

gli gnocchi *llyee nyohk·kee*	small potato dumplings
le lasagne *leh lah·sah·nyeh*	thin pasta strips layered with tomato or white sauce, meat and cheese
le linguine *leh leen·gwee·neh*	narrow, long pasta
le orecchiette *leh oh·reh·kyeht·teh*	small, shell-shaped pasta
i pansotti *ee pahn·soht·tee*	swiss chard- and herb-stuffed pasta, usually served with a walnut sauce
le pappardelle *leh pahp·pahr·dehl·leh*	long, rectangula pasta of medium width with ribbon edges
la pastina *lah pahs·tee·nah*	tiny, dried pasta used in soups
le penne *leh pehn·neh*	short, tubular pasta with angled ends
i quadrucci *ee kwah·droo·chee*	stuffed pasta squares added to soup
i rigatoni *ee ree·gah·toh·nee*	fat tubes of dried pasta with ridges
gli spaghetti *llyee spah·gheht·tee*	long thin strands of fresh pasta
le tagliatelle *leh tah·llyah·tehl·leh*	thin, long pasta with ribbon edges
i tortelli *ee tohr·tehl·lee*	stuffed rectangular or square fresh pasta
i tortellini *ee tohr·tehl·lee·nee*	small stuffed pasta nuggets
gli ziti *llyee tsee·tee*	tubular pasta
il pasticcio *pah·stee·chyoh*	pie
la pastina *lah pah·stee·nah*	tiny dried pasta used in soups

pasta... *pah•stah*	pasta with...
all'agliata *ahl•lah•llyah•tah*	hot and spicy sauce with garlic
all'Alfredo *ahl•lahl•freh•doh*	butter and parmesan cheese
all'amatriciana *ahl•lah•mah•tree•chyah•nah*	bacon and tomato
alla bolognese *ahl•lah boh•loh•nyeh•seh*	ground meat and tomato
alla boscaiola *ahl•lah boh•skah•yoh•lah*	tomatoes, butter, cheese, mushrooms, olive oil and garlic
alla carbonara *ahl•lah kahr•boh•nah•rah*	bacon and egg
fra' diavolo *frah dyah•voh•loh*	tomato with hot pepper
alla marinara *ahl•lah mah•ree•nah•rah*	tomato, olive oil and garlic
alla napoletana *ahl•lah nah•poh•leh•tah•nah*	cheese, tomatoes and herbs
al pesto *ahl peh•stoh*	ground basil, garlic, parmesan and pine nuts
al pomodoro *ahl poh•moh•doh•roh*	simple tomato sauce
alla puttanesca *ahl•lah poot•tah•neh•skah*	tomatoes, black olives, peppers, olive oil and garlic
al ragù *ahl rah•goo*	with meat

alla siciliana _ahl·lah see·chee·lyah·nah_ — provolone and eggplant

alle vongole _ahl·leh vohn·goh·leh_ — clams and tomato

la patata _lah pah·tah·tah_ — potato

la patata americana _lah pah·tah·tah ah·meh·ree·kah·nah_ — sweet potato

le patatine _leh pah·tah·tee·neh_ — potato chips [crisps]

le patatine fritte _leh pah·tah·tee·neh freet·teh_ — French fries

il paté _eel pah·teh_ — pâté

il pepe _eel peh·peh_ — pepper (seasoning)

il pepe bianco _eel peh·peh byahn·koh_ — white pepper (seasoning)

il pepe nero _eel peh·peh neh·roh_ — black pepper (seasoning)

il pepe rosso _eel peh·peh rohs·soh_ — paprika

il peperoncino _eel peh·peh·rohn·chee·noh_ — chili pepper

il peperone _eel peh·peh·roh·neh_ — pepper (vegetable)

la pera _lah peh·rah_ — pear

il persico _eel pehr·see·koh_ — fresh water perch

la pesca _lah peh·skah_ — peach

il pesce _eel peh·sheh_ — fish

il pesce spada _eel peh·sheh spah·dah_ — swordfish

il pettine di mare _eel peht·tee·neh dee mah·reh_ — scallop

il petto (di pollo) _eel peht·toh (dee pohl·loh)_ — breast (of chicken)

i pinoli _ee pee·noh·lee_ — pine nuts

il piselli _eel pee·zehl·lee_ — peas

il pesto _eel peh·stoh_ — sauce made with basil, garlic, parmesan and pinenuts

la pizza... _lah pee·tsah..._ — ...pizza

  bianca _byahn·kah_ — 'white,' without tomato sauce

  con i funghi _kohn ee foon·ghee_ — with mushrooms

  dolce _dohl·cheh_ — with a variety of sweet toppings, served as a dessert

margherita *mahr·gheh·ree·tah* — tomato, cheese and basil or oregano, named after Italy's first queen and reflecting the national colors

marinara *mah·ree·nah·rah* — with tomato sauce, garlic, capers, oregano and sometimes anchovies

napoletana *nah·poh·leh·tah·nah* — anchovies, tomatoes, cheese and sometimes capers

quattro formaggi *kwaht·troh fohr·mah·djee* — with four types of cheese

quattro stagioni *kwaht·troh stah·jyoh·nee* — 'four seasons', with tomatoes, artichokes, mushrooms, olives; plus cheese, ham and bacon

rustica *roos·tee·kah* — with ricotta, mozzarella, prosciutto, mortadella and seasonings

il pollame *eel pohl·lah·meh* — poultry
il pollo *eel pohl·loh* — chicken
la polenta *lah poh·lehn·tah* — cornmeal
la polpa di granchio *lah pohl·pah dee grahn·kyoh* — crabmeat
la polpetta *lah pohl·peht·tah* — meatball
il polpo *eel pohl·poh* — octopus
il pomodoro *eel poh·moh·doh·roh* — tomato
il pompelmo *eel pohm·pehl·moh* — grapefruit
i porcini *ee pohr·chee·nee* — porcini mushrooms
la porchetta *lah pohr·keht·tah* — suckling pig
il porro *eel pohr·roh* — leek
il porto *eel pohr·toh* — port

il prezzemolo *eel preh•tseh•moh•loh*	parsley
il prosciutto *eel proh•shyoot•toh*	ham
la prugna *lah proo•nyah*	plum
la prugna secca *lah proo•nyah sehk•kah*	prune
le puntarelle *leh poon•tah•rehl•leh*	wild chicory
la quaglia *lah kwah•llyah*	quail
il rabarbaro *eel rah•bahr•bah•roh*	rhubarb
il radicchio *eel rah•deek•kyoh*	red chicory
il ravanello *eel rah•vah•nehl•loh*	radish
la rana *lah rah•nah*	frog
la rana pescatrice *lah rah•nah peh•skah•tree•cheh*	monkfish
la rapa *lah rah•pah*	turnip
il ribes nero *eel ree•behs neh•roh*	black currant
il ribes rosso *eel ree•behs rohs•soh*	red currant
il riccio di mare *eel ree•chyoh dee mah•reh*	sea urchin
le rigaglie *leh ree•gah•llyeh*	giblet
il riso *eel ree•zoh*	rice
il risotto *eel ree•zoht•toh*	rice cooked in broth
il rosbif *eel rohz•beef*	roast beef
il rosmarino *eel rohz•mah•ree•noh*	rosemary
il rum *eel room*	rum
il salame *eel sah•lah•meh*	salami
il sale *eel sah•leh*	salt
il salmone *eel sahl•moh•neh*	salmon
la salsa *lah sahl•sah*	sauce
la salsa agrodolce *lah sahl•sah*	sweet and sour sauce
la salsa piccante *lah sahl•sah peek•kahn•teh*	hot pepper sauce
la salsa di soia *lah sahl•sah dee soh•yah*	soy sauce
la salsiccia *lah sahl•see•chyah*	sausage
la salvia *lah sahl•vyah*	sage

il sanguinaccio *eel sahn·gwee·nah·chyoh*	blood sausage
le sardine *leh sahr·dee·neh*	sardine
i savoiardi *ee sah·voh·yahr·dee*	'ladyfingers', small sponge cakes used to make tiramisu
lo scalogno *loh skah·loh·nyoh*	shallot
la scarola *lah skah·roh·lah*	escarole
lo sciroppo *loh shee·rohp·poh*	syrup
lo scotch *loh skohtch*	scotch
il sedano *eel seh·dah·noh*	celery
la segale *lah seh·gah·leh*	rye
la selvaggina *lah sehl·vah·djee·nah*	game
i semi di finocchio *ee seh·mee dee fee·nohk·kyoh*	fennel seeds
la senape *lah seh·nah·peh*	mustard
lo scombro *loh skohm·broh*	mackerel
lo sherry *loh shehr·ree*	sherry
la sogliola *lah soh·llyoh·lah*	sole
la soia *lah soh·yah*	soy [soya]
il sottaceto *eel soht·tah·cheh·toh*	pickle
la spalla *lah spahl·lah*	shoulder
le spezie *leh speh·tsyeh*	spices
lo spezzatino *loh speh·tsah·tee·noh*	meat stew
gli spinaci *llyee spee·nah·chee*	spinach
la spremuta *lah spreh·muh·tah*	fresh-squeezed juice
lo stinco *loh steen·koh*	shank
lo strutto *loh stroot·toh*	lard
il succo *eel sook·koh*	juice
il tacchino *eel tahk·kee·noh*	turkey
il tartufo *eel tahr·too·foh*	truffles
il tè *eel teh*	tea
il timo *eel tee·moh*	thyme

il tofu *eel toh•foo*	tofu
il tonno *eel tohn•noh*	tuna
il torrone *eel tohr•roh•neh*	nougat
la torta *lah tohr•tah*	cake
la triglia *lah tree•llyah*	red mullet
la trippa *lah treep•pah*	tripe
la trota *lah troh•tah*	trout
il tuorlo *eel twohr•loh*	egg yolk
l'uovo *lwoh•voh*	egg
l'uva *loo•vah*	grape
l'uva spina *loo•vah spee•nah*	gooseberry
l'uvetta *loo•veht•tah*	raisin
la vaniglia *lah vah•nee•llyah*	vanilla
il vermouth *eel vehr•mooth*	vermouth
la verdura *lah vehr•doo•rah*	vegetable
il vino *eel vee•noh*	wine
il vino da dessert *eel vee•noh dah dehs•sehrt*	dessert wine
il vitello *eel vee•tehl•loh*	veal
la vodka *lah vohd•kah*	vodka
la vongola *lah vohn•goh•lah*	clam
il wafer *eel vah•fehr*	waffle
il whisky *eel whee•skee*	whisky
il wurstel *eel voor•stehl*	hot dog
lo yogurt *loh yoh•goort*	yogurt
lo zafferano *loh dzahf•feh•rah•noh*	saffron
lo zenzero *loh dzehn•dzeh•roh*	ginger
la zucca *lah dzook•kah*	squash
lo zucchero *loh dzook•keh•roh*	sugar
la zucchina *lah dzook•kee•nah*	zucchini [courgette]
la zuppa *lah dzoop•pah*	soup

People

Conversation   101
Romance   108

ESSENTIAL

Hello!/Hi!	**Salve!/Ciao!**	_sahl_•veh/_chah_•oh
How are you?	**Come sta?**	_koh_•meh stah
Fine, thanks.	**Bene, grazie.**	_beh_•neh _grah_•tsyeh
Excuse me!	**Scusi!**	_skoo_•zee
Do you speak English?	**Parla inglese?**	_pahr_•lah een•_gleh_•zeh
What's your name?	**Come si chiama?**	_koh_•meh see _kyah_•mah
My name is...	**Mi chiamo...**	mee _kyah_•moh...
Nice to meet you.	**Piacere.**	pyah•_cheh_•reh
Where are you from?	**Di dov'è?**	dee doh•_veh_
I'm American.	**Sono americano _m_/americana _f._**	
	soh•noh ah•meh•ree•_kah_•noh/ah•meh•ree•_kah_•nah	
I'm English.	**Sono inglese.**	_soh_•noh een•_gleh_•zeh
What do you do for a living?	**Cosa fa?**	_koh_•zah fah
I work for...	**Lavoro per...**	lah•_voh_•roh pehr...
I'm a student.	**Studio.**	_stoo_•dyoh
I'm retired.	**Sono in pensione.**	_soh_•noh een pehn•_syoh_•neh
Do you like...?	**Le piace...?**	leh _pyah_•cheh...
Goodbye.	**Arrivederla.**	ahr•ree•veh•_dehr_•lah
See you later.	**A dopo.**	ah _doh_•poh

Language Difficulties

Do you speak English?	**Parla inglese?**	_pahr_•lah een•_gleh_•zeh
Does anyone here speak English?	**Qualcuno parla inglese?**	kwahl•_koo_•noh _pahr_•lah een•_gleh_•zeh

Italians have many greetings. The following are the most commonly used forms and when to use them.

buongiorno: literally, good day; this greeting is used from morning to mid-afternoon

salve: a formal hello

ciao: an informal hi or bye

buon pomeriggio: good afternoon

buonasera: good evening; used from late afternoon until late in the evening

buonanotte: good night; used late in the evening or at bedtime

arrivederla: formal goodbye

arrivederci: informal goodbye

I don't speak (much) Italian.	**Non parlo (molto bene l') italiano.** nohn _pahr_•loh (_mohl_•toh _beh_•neh l) ee•tah•_lyah_•noh
Can you speak more slowly?	**Può parlare più lentamente?** pwoh pahr•_lah_•reh pyoo lehn•tah•_mehn_•teh
Can you repeat that?	**Può ripetere?** pwoh ree•_peh_•teh•reh
Excuse me?	**Come?** _koh_•meh
What was that?	**Cosa ha detto?** _koh_•zah ah _deht_•toh
Can you spell it?	**Come si scrive?** _koh_•meh see _skree_•veh
Can you write it down?	**Me lo può scrivere?** meh loh pwo _skree_•veh•reh
Can you translate this into English for me?	**Può tradurlo in inglese?** pwoh trah•_door_•loh een een•_gleh_•zeh
What does… mean?	**Che significa…?** keh see•_nyee_•fee•kah…
I understand.	**Capisco.** kah•_pee_•skoh
I don't understand.	**Non capisco.** nohn kah•_pee_•skoh
Do you understand?	**Capisce?** kah•_pee_•sheh

Making Friends

Hello!	**Salve!** _sahl_•veh
Good morning.	**Buongiorno.** bwohn•_jyohr_•noh
Good afternoon.	**Buon pomeriggio.** bwohn poh•meh•_ree_•djoh
Good evening.	**Buonasera.** bwoh•nah•_seh_•rah
My name is…	**Mi chiamo…** mee _kyah_•moh…
What's your name?	**Come si chiama?** _koh_•meh see _kyah_•mah
I'd like to introduce you to…	**Le presento…** leh preh•_zehn_•toh…
Pleased to meet you.	**Piacere.** pyah•_cheh_•reh
How are you?	**Come sta?** _koh_•meh stah
Fine, thanks. And you?	**Bene, grazie. E Lei?** _beh_•neh _grah_•tsyeh eh lay

Signore (Mr.), **Signora** (Mrs.), **Signorina** (Miss) and professional titles - **Dottore** (Dr.), **Professore** (Professor) - are frequently used, even when you don't know the person's last name. When trying to get someone's attention, you don't have to include his or her title; a simple **Scusi!** (formal) or **Scusa!** (informal) is sufficient.

YOU MAY HEAR...

Parlo poco inglese. _pahr_•loh _poh_•koh
een•_gleh_•zeh

I only speak a little
English.

Non parlo inglese. nohn _pahr_•loh
een•_gleh_•zeh

I don't speak English.

Travel Talk

I'm here...	**Sono qui...** _soh_•noh kwee...
on business	**per lavoro** pehr lah•_voh_•roh
on vacation	**in vacanza** een vah•_kahn_•tsah
studying	**per studio** pehr _stoo_•dyoh
I'm staying for...	**Rimango...** ree•_mahn_•goh...
I've been here...	**Sono qui da...** _soh_•noh kwee dah...
a day	**un giorno** oon _jyohr_•noh
a week	**una settimana** _oo_•nah seht•tee•_mah_•nah
a month	**un mese** oon _meh_•zeh
Where are you from?	**Di dove sei?** dee doh•_veh_ seh•ee
I'm from...	**Sono di...** _soh_•noh dee...

For Numbers, see page 167.

Personal

Who are you with?	**Con chi è?** *kohn kee ee*
I'm here alone.	**Sono da solo** *m* **/sola** *f soh*•*noh dah* <u>*soh*</u>•*loh/*<u>*soh*</u>•*lah*
I'm with my...	**Sono con...** *soh*•*noh kohn...*
husband/wife	**mio marito** *m* **/mia moglie** *f* <u>*mee*</u>•*oh mah*•<u>*ree*</u>•*toh/* <u>*mee*</u>•*ah moh*•*llyeh*
boyfriend/ girlfriend	**il mio ragazzo** *m* **/la mia ragazza** *f eel* <u>*mee*</u>•*oh rah*•<u>*gah*</u>•*tsoh/lah mee*•*ah rah*•<u>*gah*</u>•*tsah*
a friend	**un amico** *m* **/un'amica** *f oon ah*•<u>*mee*</u>•*koh/ oo*•*nah*•<u>*mee*</u>•*kah*
friends	**degli amici** *m* **/delle amiche** *f* <u>*deh*</u>•*llyee ah*•<u>*mee*</u>•*chee/dehl*•*leh ah*•<u>*mee*</u>•*keh*
a colleague	**un** *m* **/una** *f collega oon/*<u>*oo*</u>•*nah kohl*•<u>*leh*</u>•*gah*
colleagues	**dei colleghi** *m* **/delle colleghe** *f day kohl*•<u>*leh*</u>•*ghee/ deh*•*leh kohl*•<u>*leh*</u>•*gheh*
When's your birthday?	**Quando è il suo compleanno?** *kwahn*•*doh eh eel* <u>*soo*</u>•*oh kohm*•*pleh*•<u>*ahn*</u>•*noh*
How old are you?	**Quanti anni ha?** *kwahn*•*tee* <u>*ahn*</u>•*nee ah*
I'm...years old.	**Ho...anni.** *oh...* <u>*ahn*</u>•*nee*
Are you married?	**È sposato** *m* **/sposata** *f?* *eh spoh*•<u>*zah*</u>•*toh/ spoh*•<u>*zah*</u>•*tah*
I'm...	**Sono...** *soh*•*noh...*
single	**single** <u>*seen*</u>•*guhl*
engaged	**fidanzato** *m* **/ fidanzata** *f fee*•*dan*•<u>*zah*</u>•*toh/ fee*•*dan*•<u>*zah*</u>•*tah/*
married	**sposato** *m* **/sposata** *f spoh*•<u>*zah*</u>•*toh/spoh*•<u>*zah*</u>•*tah*
divorced	**divorziato** *m* **/divorziata** *f dee*•*vohr*•<u>*tsyah*</u>•*toh/ dee*•*vohr*•<u>*tsyah*</u>•*tah*
separated	**separato** *m* **/separata** *f seh*•*pah*•<u>*rah*</u>•*toh/ seh*•*pah*•<u>*rah*</u>•*tah*
widowed	**vedovo** *m* **/vedova** *f* <u>*veh*</u>•*doh*•*voh/*<u>*veh*</u>•*doh*•*vah*

A handshake is a common gesture among strangers or in formal settings. Traditionally, it is expected that a woman be the first to offer her hand. A kiss on both cheeks is used among friends and relatives. A nod and a smile suffice when greeting members of a group of people.

I have a boyfriend/ girlfriend.	**Ho un ragazzo/una ragazza.** *oh oon rah•gah•tsoh/ oo•nah rah•gah•tsah*
Do you have children/ grandchildren?	**Ha figli/nipoti?** *ah fee•llyee/nee•poh•tee*

For Numbers, see page 167.

Work & School

What do you do for a living?	**Cosa fa?** *koh•zah fah*
What are you studying?	**Cosa studia?** *koh•zah stoo•dyah*
I'm studying Italian.	**Studio italiano.** *stoo•dyoh ee•tah•lyah•noh*
I...	**Io...** *ee•oh...*
work full-time/ part-time	**lavoro full-time/part-time** *lah•voh•roh fool•tym/pahrt•tym*
am unemployed	**sono disoccupato m /disoccupata f** *soh•noh dee•zohk•koo•pah•toh/dee•zohk•koo•pah•tah*
work at home	**lavoro a casa** *lah•voh•roh ah kah•zah*
Who do you work for?	**Per chi lavora?** *pehr kee lah•voh•rah*
I work for...	**Lavoro per...** *lah•voh•roh pehr...*
Here's my business card.	**Ecco il mio biglietto da visita.** *ehk•koh eel mee•oh bee•llyeht•toh dah vee•zee•tah*

For Business Travel, see page 141.

Weather

What's the forecast?	**Come sono le previsioni?** _koh_•meh _soh_•noh _leh preh•vee•_zyoh_•nee
What beautiful/ terrible weather!	**Che bel/brutto tempo!** _keh behl/_broot_•toh _tehm_•poh
It's...	**Fa...** _fah..._
cool/warm.	**fresco/caldo.** _freh_•skoh/_kahl_•doh
It's cold/hot.	**freddo/caldo.** _fah_ _frehd_•doh/_kahl_•doh
It's rainy.	**Piove.** _pyoh_•veh
It's sunny.	**C'è il sole.** _cheh eel _soh_•leh
It's snowy.	**Nevica.** _neh_•vee•kah
It's icy.	**Gela.** _jeh_•lah
Do I need a jacket/ an umbrella?	**Devo prendere una giacca/un ombrello?** _deh_•voh _prehn_•deh•reh _oo_•nah _jyahk_•kah/ _oon ohm_•_brehl_•loh

For Temperature, see page 173.

Romance

ESSENTIAL

Would you like to go out for a drink/dinner?	**Le va di andare a bere qualcosa/cena?** *leh vah dee ahn-dah-reh ah beh-reh kwahl-koh-zah/cheh-nah*
What are your plans for tonight/tomorrow?	**Che programmi ha per stasera/domani?** *keh proh-grahm-mee ah pehr stah-seh-rah/doh-mah-nee*
Can I have your number?	**Mi dà il suo numero?** *mee dah eel soo-oh noo-meh-roh*
Can I buy you a drink?	**Posso offrirle qualcosa?** *pohs-soh ohf-freer-leh kwahl-koh-zah*
I like you.	**Mi piaci.** *mee pyah-chee*
I love you.	**Ti amo.** *tee ah-moh*

The Dating Game

Would you like to go out for a coffee/drink?	**Le va di andare a prendere un caffè/ bicchierino?** *leh vah dee ahn-dah-reh ah prehn-deh-reh oon kahf-feh/bee-kyeh-ree-noh*
Would you like to go to dinner?	**Le va di andare a cena?** *leh vah dee ahn-dah-reh ah cheh-nah*
What are your plans for…?	**Che programmi ha per…?** *keh proh-grahm-mee ah pehr…*
today	**oggi** *oh-dgee*
tonight	**stasera** *stah-seh-rah*
tomorrow	**domani** *doh-mah-nee*
this weekend	**questo weekend** *kweh-stoh week-ehnd*

Where would you like to go?	**Dove le va di andare?** _doh_•veh leh vah dee ahn•_dah_•reh
I'd like to go to…	**Vorrei andare a…** vohr•_ray_ ahn•_dah_•reh ah…
Do you like…?	**Le piace…?** leh _pyah_•cheh…
Can I have your number/e-mail?	**Mi dà il suo numero/la sua e-mail?** mee dah eel _soo_•oh _noo_•meh•roh/lah _soo_•ah _ee_•mayl
Are you on Facebook/Twitter?	**È su Facebook/Twitter?** eh soo feh•eez•book/tweet•tehr
Can I join you?	**Mi posso sedere?** mee pohs•soh seh•_deh_•reh
You're very attractive.	**È molto attraente.** eh _mohl_•toh aht•trah•_ehn_•teh
Let's go somewhere quieter.	**Andiamo in un posto più tranquillo.** ahn•_dyah_•moh een oon _poh_•stoh pyoo trahn•_kweel_•loh

For Communications, see page 47.

Accepting & Rejecting

I'd love to.	**Mi piacerebbe moltissimo.** mee pyah•cheh•_rehb_•beh mohl•_tees_•see•moh
Where should we meet?	**Dove ci vediamo?** _doh_•veh chee veh•_dyah_•moh
I'll meet you at the bar/your hotel.	**Vediamoci al bar/nel suo hotel.** veh•_dyah_•moh•chee ahl bahr/nehl _soo_•oh oh•_tehl_
I'll come by at…	**Passo alle…** _pahs_•soh _ahl_•leh…
What is your address?	**Mi dà il suo indirizzo?** mee dah eel _soo_•oh een•dee•_ree_•tsoh
I'm busy.	**Ho da fare.** oh dah _fah_•reh
I'm not interested.	**Non m'interessa.** nohn meen•teh•_rehs_•sah
Leave me alone.	**Mi lasci in pace.** mee _lah_•shee een _pah_•cheh
Stop bothering me!	**Smetta d'infastidirmi!** _smeht_•tah deen•_fah_•stee•_deer_•mee

For Time, see page 169

Getting Intimate

Can I hug you/ kiss you?	**Posso abbracciarti/baciarti?** _pohs•soh ahb•brah•<u>chyahr</u>•tee/bah•<u>chyahr</u>•tee_
Yes.	**Sì.** _see_
No.	**No.** _noh_
Stop!	**Basta!** _bah•stah_
I like you.	**Mi piaci.** _mee <u>pyah</u>•chee_
I love you.	**Ti amo.** _tee <u>ah</u>•moh_

Sexual Preferences

Are you gay?	**Sei gay?** _say gay_
I'm…	**Sono…** <u>soh</u>•noh…
heterosexual	**eterosessuale** _eh•teh•roh•sehs•<u>swah</u>•leh_
homosexual	**omosessuale** _oh•moh•sehs•<u>swah</u>•leh_
bisexual	**bisex** _bee•<u>sehks</u>_
Do you like men/ women?	**Ti piacciono gli uomini/le donne?** _tee <u>pyah</u>•chyoh•noh llyee <u>woh</u>•mee•nee/leh <u>dohn</u>•neh_

Leisure Time

Sightseeing	112
Shopping	116
Sport & Leisure	131
Going Out	137

ESSENTIAL

Where's the tourist information office?	**Dov'è l'ufficio informazioni turistiche?** *doh-veh loof-fee-chyoh een-fohr-mah-tsyoh-nee too-ree-stee-keh*
What are the main sights?	**Cosa c'è da vedere?** *koh-zah ceh dah veh-deh-reh*
Do you offer tours in English?	**Ci sono visite guidate in inglese?** *chee soh-noh vee-zee-teh gwee-dah-teh een een-gleh-zeh*
Can I have a map/guide?	**Mi può dare una cartina/guida?** *mee pwoh dah-reh oo-nah kahr-tee-nah/gwee-dah*

Tourist Information

Do you have information on…?	**Avete informazioni su…?** *ah-veh-teh een-fohr-mah-tsyoh-nee soo…*
Can you recommend…?	**Può consigliarmi…?** *pwoh kohn-see-llyahr-mee…*
a bus tour	**una gita in pullman** *oo-nah jee-tah een pool-mahn*
an excursion to…	**un'escursione a…** *oo-neh-skoor-syoh-neh ah…*
a sightseeing tour	**una gita turistica** *oo-nah jee-tah too-ree-stee-kah*

L'ufficio informazioni turistiche (tourist information office) can be found in almost every town; some may be located at the airport or main train station. Get local events listings, maps, transportation schedules and more at any of these offices.

On Tour

I'd like to go on the excursion to…	**Vorrei partecipare alla gita per…** *vohr•<u>ray</u> pahr•teh•chee•<u>pah</u>•reh <u>ahl</u>•lah <u>jee</u>•tah pehr…*
When's the next tour?	**Quando è la prossima gita?** *<u>kwahn</u>•doh eh lah <u>prohs</u>•see•mah <u>jee</u>•tah*
Are there tours in English?	**Ci sono visite guidate in inglese?** *chee <u>soh</u>•noh <u>vee</u>•zee•teh gwee•<u>dah</u>•teh een een•<u>gleh</u>•zeh*
Is there an English guide book/audio guide?	**C'è una guida/un'audio guida in inglese?** *cheh <u>oo</u>•nah <u>gwee</u>•dah/oo•<u>now</u>•dyoh <u>gwee</u>•dah een een•<u>gleh</u>•zeh*
What time do we leave/return?	**A che ora si torna?** *ah keh <u>oh</u>•rah see <u>tohr</u>•nah*
We'd like to see…	**Vorremmo vedere…** *vohr•<u>rehm</u>•moh veh•<u>deh</u>•reh…*
Can we stop here…?	**Possiamo fermarci…?** *pohs•<u>syah</u>•moh fehr•<u>mahr</u>•chee…*
to take photos	**per fare qualche foto** *pehr <u>fah</u>•reh <u>kwahl</u>•keh <u>foh</u>•toh*
for souvenirs	**per comprare qualche souvenir** *pehr kohm•<u>prah</u>•reh <u>kwahl</u>•keh soo•veh•<u>neer</u>*
for the toilets	**per andare in bagno** *pehr ahn•<u>dah</u>•reh een <u>bah</u>•nyoh*
Is it disabled-accessible?	**È accessibile ai disabili?** *eh ah•chehs•<u>see</u>•bee•leh <u>ah</u>•ee dee•<u>zah</u>•bee•lee*

Seeing the Sights

Where is/Where are...?	**Dov'è/Dove sono...?** doh-_veh_/_doh_-veh _soh_-noh...
the battleground	**il campo di battaglia?** _eel kahm_-poh dee baht-tah-_llyah_?
the botanical garden	**il giardino botanico** _eel jyahr_-dee-_dee_-noh boh-_tah_-nee-koh
the castle	**il castello** eel kah-_stehl_-loh
the downtown area	**il centro** eel _chehn_-troh
the fountain	**la fontana** lah fohn-_tah_-nah
the library	**la biblioteca** lah bee-blyoh-_teh_-kah
the market	**il mercato** eel mehr-_kah_-toh
the museum	**il museo** eel moo-_zeh_-oh
the old town	**la città vecchia** lah cheet-_tah_ vehk-kyah
the opera house	**il teatro dell'opera** eel teh-_ah_-troh deh-_loh_-peh-rah
the palace	**il palazzo** eel pah-_lah_-tsoh
the park	**il parco** eel _pahr_-koh
the ruins	**le rovine** leh roh-_vee_-neh
the shopping area	**i negozi** ee neh-_goh_-tzee
the town hall	**il comune** eel koh-_moo_-neh
the town square	**la piazza principale** lah _pyah_-tsah preen-chee-_pah_-leh
Can you show me on the map?	**Può indicarmelo sulla cartina?** pwoh een-dee-_kahr_-meh-loh _sool_-lah kahr-_tee_-nah
It's...	**È...** eh...
amazing	**meraviglioso** meh-rah-vee-_llyoh_-zoh
beautiful	**bellissimo** behl-_lees_-see-moh
boring	**noioso** noh-_yoh_-zoh
interesting	**interessante** een-teh-rehs-_sahn_-teh
magnificent	**magnifico** mah-_nyee_-fee-koh

romantic	**romantico** roh•_mahn_•tee•koh
strange	**strano** _strah_•noh
stunning	**fenomenale** feh•noh•meh•_nah_•leh
terrible	**terribile** tehr•_ree_•bee•leh
ugly	**brutto** _broot_•toh
I (don't) like it.	**(Non) Mi piace.** (nohn) mee _pyah_•cheh

For Asking Directions, see page 33.

Religious Sites

Where's…?	**Dov'è…?** doh•_veh_…
the cathedral	**la cattedrale** lah kaht•teh•_drah_•leh
the Catholic/ Protestant church	**la chiesa cattolica/protestante** lah _kyeh_•zah kaht•_toh_•lee•kah/proh•teh•_stahn_•teh
the mosque	**la moschea** lah moh•_skeh_•ah
the shrine	**il santuario** eel sahn•_twah_•ryoh
the synagogue	**la sinagoga** lah see•nah•_goh_•gah
the temple	**il tempio** eel _tehm_•pyoh
What time is the mass/service?	**A che ora è la messa/il servizio?** ah keh _oh_•rah eh lah _mehs_•sah/eel sehr•_vee_•tsyoh

Shopping

ESSENTIAL

Where's the market/ mall [shopping centre]?	**Dov'è il mercato/centro commerciale?** *doh·veh eel mehr·kah·toh/chehn·troh kohm·mehr·chyah·leh*
I'm just looking.	**Sto solo guardando.** *stoh soh·loh gwahr·dahn·doh*
Can you help me?	**Può aiutarmi?** *pwoh ah·yoo·tahr·mee*
I'm being helped.	**Mi stanno servendo.** *mee stahn·noh sehr·vehn·doh*
How much?	**Quant'è?** *kwahn·teh*
That one, please.	**Quello, per favore.** *kwehl·loh pehr fah·voh·reh*
That's all.	**Basta così.** *bah·stah koh·zee*
Where can I pay?	**Dove posso pagare?** *doh·veh pohs·soh pah·gah·reh*
I'll pay in cash/ by credit card.	**Pago in contanti/con carta di credito.** *pah·goh een kohn·tahn·tee/kohn kahr·tah dee kreh·dee·toh*
A receipt, please.	**Una ricevuta, per favore.** *oo·nah ree·cheh·voo·tah pehr fah·voh·reh*

At the Shops

Where's...?	**Dov'è...?** *doh·veh...*
the antiques store	**un negozio di antiquariato** *oon neh·goh·tsyoh dee ahn·tee·kwah·ryah·toh*
the bakery	**una panetteria** *oo·nah pah·neht·teh·ree·ah*
the bank	**una banca** *oo·nah bahn·kah*
the bookstore	**una libreria** *oo·nah lee·breh·ree·ah*
the camera store	**un negozio di fotografia** *oon neh·goh·tsyoh dee foh·toh·grah·fee·ah*
the clothing store	**un negozio di abbigliamento** *oon neh·goh·tsyoh dee ahb·bee·llyah·mehn·toh*

the delicatessen	**un negozio di gastronomia** *oon neh·<u>goh</u>·tsyoh dee gahs·troh·noh·<u>mee</u>·ah*
the department store	**un grande magazzino** *oon <u>grahn</u>·deh mah·gah·<u>dzee</u>·noh*
the gift shop	**un negozio di oggettistica** *oon neh·<u>goh</u>·tsyoh dee oh·djeht·<u>tee</u>·stee·kah*
the health food store	**un'erboristeria** *oo·nehr·boh·ree·steh·<u>ree</u>·ah*
the jeweler	**una gioiellieria** <u>oo</u>·nah jyoh·yehl·lyeh·<u>ree</u>·ah
the liquor store [off-licence]	**un'enoteca** *oo·neh·noh·<u>teh</u>·kah*
the market	**un mercato** *oon mehr·<u>kah</u>·toh*
the music store	**il negozio di musica?** *eel neh·goh·tsyoh dee moo·see·kah?*
the pastry shop	**una pasticceria** <u>oo</u>·nah pah·stee·cheh·<u>ree</u>·ah
the pharmacy [chemist]	**una farmacia** <u>oo</u>·nah fahr·mah·<u>chee</u>·ah
the produce [grocery] store	**il fruttivendolo** *eel froot·tee·vehn·<u>doh</u>·loh*
the shoe store	**un negozio di calzature** *oon neh·<u>goh</u>·tsyoh dee kahl·tsah·<u>too</u>·reh*
the shopping mall [shopping centre]	**un centro commerciale** *oon <u>chehn</u>·troh kohm·mehr·<u>chyah</u>·leh*
the souvenir store	**un negozio di souvenir** *oon neh·<u>goh</u>·tsyoh dee soo·veh·<u>neer</u>*
the supermarket	**un supermercato** *oon soo·pehr·mehr·<u>kah</u>·toh*
the tobacconist	**un tabaccaio** *oon tah·bahk·<u>kah</u>·yoh*
the toy store	**un negozio di giocattoli** *oon neh·<u>goh</u>·tsyoh dee jyoh·<u>kaht</u>·toh·lee*

Ask an Assistant

When do you open/close?	**Quando aprite/chiudete?** _kwahn•doh ah•<u>pree</u>•teh/ kyoo•<u>deh</u>•teh_
Where is/Where are…?	**Dov'è/Dove sono…?** _doh•<u>veh</u>/<u>doh</u>•veh <u>soh</u>•noh…_
the cashier	**la cassa** _lah <u>kahs</u>•sah_
the escalator	**le scale mobili** _leh <u>skah</u>•leh <u>moh</u>•bee•lee_
the elevator [lift]	**l'ascensore** _lah•shehn•<u>soh</u>•reh_
the fitting room	**il camerino** _eel kah•meh•<u>ree</u>•noh_
the store directory	**la piantina del negozio** _lah pyahn•<u>tee</u>•nah dehl neh•<u>goh</u>•tsyoh_
Can you help me?	**Può aiutarmi?** _pwoh ah•yoo•<u>tahr</u>•mee_
I'm just looking.	**Sto solo guardando.** _stoh <u>soh</u>•loh gwahr•<u>dahn</u>•doh_
I'm being helped.	**Mi stanno servendo.** _mee <u>stahn</u>•noh sehr•<u>vehn</u>•doh_
Do you have…?	**Avete…?** _ah•<u>veh</u>•teh…_
Can you show me…?	**Può mostrarmi…?** _pwoh moh•<u>strahr</u>•mee_
Can you ship it/ wrap it?	**Può spedirlo/incartarlo?** _pwoh speh•<u>deer</u>•loh/ een•kahr•<u>tahr</u>•loh_
How much?	**Quant'è?** _kwahn•<u>teh</u>_
That's all.	**Basta così.** _<u>bah</u>•stah koh•<u>zee</u>_

For Clothing, see page 124.

Personal Preferences

I'd like something…	**Vorrei qualcosa…** *vohr·ray kwahl·koh·zah…*
cheap/expensive	**di più economico/caro** *dee pyoo eh·koh·noh·mee·koh/kah·roh*
larger/smaller	**di più grande/piccolo** *dee pyoo grahn·deh/peek·koh·loh*
from this region	**di tipico di questa zona** *dee tee·pee·koh dee kweh·stah dzoh·nah*
Around…euros.	**Intorno ai…euro.** *een·tohr·noh ah·ee…eh·oo·roh*
Is it real?	**È vero?** *eh veh·roh*
Can you show me…?	**Mi fa vedere…?** *mee fah veh·deh·reh*
That's not quite what I want.	**Non è proprio quello che volevo.** *nohn eh proh·pryoh kwehl·loh keh voh·leh·voh*
No, I don't like it.	**No, non mi piace.** *noh nohn mee pyah·cheh*
It's too expensive.	**È troppo caro.** *eh trohp·poh kah·roh*
I have to think about it.	**Devo pensarci.** *deh·voh pehn·sahr·chee*
I'll take it.	**Lo prendo.** *loh prehn·doh*

YOU MAY SEE…

APERTO	open
CHIUSO	closed
ENTRATA	entrance
CAMERINO	fitting room
CASSA	cashier
SOLO CONTANTI	cash only
SI ACCETTANO CARTE DI CREDITO	credit cards accepted
ORARIO D'APERTURA	business hours
USCITA	exit

YOU MAY HEAR...

Posso aiutarla? _pohs·soh ah·yoo·tahr lah_ — Can I help you?

Un momento. _oon moh·mehn·toh_ — One moment.

Che cosa desidera? _keh koh·zah deh·zee·deh·rah_ — What would you like?

Altro? _ahl·troh_ — Anything else?

Paying & Bargaining

How much?	**Quant'è?** _kwahn·teh_
I'll pay...	**Pago...** _pah·goh..._
in cash	**in contanti** _een kohn·tahn·tee_
by credit card	**con carta di credito** _kohn kahr·tah dee kreh·dee·toh_
by travelers check [cheque]	**con un travel cheque** _kohn oon trah·vehl chehk_
Can I use...?	**Posso usare...?** _pohs·soh oo·zah·reh..._
this ATM/debit card	**questo bancomat** _kweh·stoh bahn·koh·maht_
this credit card	**questa carta di credito** _kweh·stah kahr·tah dee kreh·dee·toh_
this gift card	**questo buono** _kweh·stoh bwoh·noh_
this prepaid card	**questa carta prepagata** _kweh·stah kahr·tah preh·pah·gah·tah_

Cash is still the most widely used and preferred method of payment, followed by **bancomat** (ATM cards). Credit cards are widely accepted, especially for larger purchases. Traveler's checks are accepted at most establishments.

How do I use this machine?	**Come si usa questa macchina?** _koh·meh see oo·zah kweh·stah mahk·kee·nah_
How much is left on the card?	**Quanto credito c'è sulla carta?** _kwahn·toh kreh·dee·toh cheh sool·lah kahr·tah_
A receipt, please.	**Una ricevuta, per favore.** _oo·nah ree·cheh·voo·tah pehr fah·voh·reh_

I'll give you…	**Le posso dare…** _leh pohs·soh dah·reh…_
I have only…euros.	**Ho solo…euro.** _oh soh·loh…eh·oo·roh_
Is that your best price?	**È il prezzo migliore che può farmi?** _eh eel preh·tsoh mee·llyoh·reh keh pwoh fahr·mee_

YOU MAY HEAR…

Come preferisce pagare? _koh·meh preh·feh·ree·sheh pah·gah·reh_	How are you paying?
La sua carta di credito è stata rifiutata. _lah soo·ah kahr·tah dee kreh·dee·toh eh stah·tah ree·fyoo·tah·tah_	Your credit card has been declined.
Un documento, per favore. _oon doh·koo·mehn·toh pehr fah·voh·reh_	ID, please.
Non accettiamo carte di credito. _nohn ah·cheht·tyah·moh kahr·teh dee kreh·dee·toh_	We don't accept credit cards.
Solo contanti, per favore. _soh·loh kohn·tahn·tee pehr fah·voh·reh_	Cash only, please.
Non ha spiccioli/banconote più piccole? _nohn ah spee·chyoh·lee/bahn·koh·noh·teh pyoo peek·koh·leh_	Do you have change/small bills [notes]?
Grazie. _grah·tsyeh_	Thank you.
Buona giornata! _bwoh·nah jyohr·nah·tah_	Have a nice day!

| That's too much. | **È troppo.** *eh trohp•poh* |
| Can you give me a discount? | **Mi fa un po' di sconto?** *mee fah oon poh dee skohn•toh* |

For Numbers, see page 167.

Making a Complaint

This is broken.	**È rotto** *m* **/rotta** *f eh roht•toh/roh•tah*
I bought it yesterday.	**L'ho comprato** *m* **/comprata** *f* **ieri.** *loh kohm•prah•toh/kohm•prah•tah yeh•ree*
I'd like...	**Vorrei...** *vohr•ray...*
to exchange this	**cambiarlo** *m* **/cambiarla** *f kahm•byahr•loh/ kahm•byahr•lah*
a refund	**un rimborso** *oon reem•bohr•soh*
to see the manager	**parlare con il responsabile** *pahr•lah•reh kohn eel reh•spohn•sah•bee•leh*

Services

Can you recommend...?	**Può consigliarmi...?** *pwoh kohn•see•llyahr•mee...*
a barber	**un barbiere** *oon bahr•byeh•reh*
a dry cleaner	**il lavasecco** *eel lah•vah•sehk•koh*
a hairstylist	**un parrucchiere** *oon pahr•rook•kyeh•reh*
a laundromat [launderette]	**una lavanderia a gettone** *oo•nah lah•vahn•deh•ree•ah ah jeht•toh•neh*
a nail salon	**un salone di bellezza** *oon sah•loh•neh dee beh•leh•tsah*
a spa	**una stazione termali** *oo•nah stah•tsyoh•neh tehr•mah•lee*
a travel agency	**un'agenzia di viaggi** *oo•nah•jehn•tsee•ah dee vyah•djee*
Can you...this?	**Mi può...questo** *m* **/questa** *f* **?** *mee pwoh... kweh•stoh/kweh•stah*
alter	**cambiare** *kahm•byah•reh*
clean	**pulire** *poo•lee•reh*

fix [mend]	**riparare** _ree·pah·rah·reh_
press	**stirare** _stee·rah·reh_
When will it be ready?	**Per quando è pronto _m_/pronta _f_?** _pehr kwahn·doh eh prohn·toh/prohn·tah_

Hair & Beauty

I'd like...	**Vorrei...** _vohr·ray_...
an appointment for today/ tomorrow	**un appuntamento per oggi/domani** _oon ahp·poon·tah·mehn·toh pehr oh·djee/doh·mah·nee_
some color/ highlights	**fare il colore/i colpi di sole** _fah·reh eel koh·loh·reh/ee kohl·pee dee soh·leh_
my hair styled/ blow-dried	**fare la piega/asciugare** _fah·reh lah pyeh·gah/ah·shoo·gah·reh_
a haircut	**fare il taglio** _fah·reh eel tah·llyoh_
a bikini wax	**fare la ceretta all'inguine** _fah·reh lah cheh·reht·tah ahl·leen·gwee·neh_
a facial	**fare la pulizia del viso** _fah-reh lah poo·lee·tsee·ah dehl vee·soh_
a manicure/ pedicure	**fare un manicure/pedicure** _fah-reh oon mah·nee·koor·eh/peh·dee·koor·eh_
a massage	**fare un massaggio** _fah·reh oon mahs·sah·djoh_
a trim	**dare una spuntatina** _dah·reh oo·nah spoon·tah·tee·nah_
Not too short.	**Non troppo corti.** _nohn trohp·poh kohr·tee_
Shorter here.	**Più corti qui.** _pyoo kohr·tee kwee_
Do you offer...?	**Fate...?** _fah·teh_...
acupuncture	**l'agopuntura** _lah·goh·poon·too·rah_
aromatherapy	**l'aromaterapia** _lah·roh·mah·teh·rah·pee·ah_
oxygen treatment	**l'ossigeno terapia** _lohs·see·jeh·noh teh·rah·pee·ah_
Do you have a sauna?	**C'è la sauna?** _cheh lah sah·ow·nah_

Italy is well-known for its **stazioni termale** (spas), which can
be found throughout the country. Many of these spas are located
near thermal springs and offer medicinal treatments. Some are day
spas and others are hotel spas, which may offer weekend packages.
Tipping is optional, as service is usually included.

Antiques

How old is it?	**Di quando è?** dee _kwahn_·doh eh
Do you have anything from the...period?	**Avete qualcosa del periodo...?** ah·_veh_·teh kwahl·_koh_·zah dehl peh·_ryoh_·doh...
Do I have to fill out any forms?	**Devo riempire un modulo?** _deh_·voh ree·ehm·_pee_·reh oon _moh_·doo·loh
Is there a certificate of authenticity?	**Ha il certificato di autenticità?** ah eel chehr·tee·fee·_kah_·toh dee ow·tehn·tee·chee·_tah_

Clothing

I'd like...	**Vorrei...** vohr·_ray_...
Can I try this on?	**Posso provarlo?** _pohs_·soh proh·_vahr_·loh
It doesn't fit.	**Non mi va bene.** nohn mee vah _beh_·neh
It's too...	**È troppo...** eh _trohp_·poh...
big/small	**grande/piccolo** _grahn_·deh/_peek_·koh·loh
short/long	**corto/lungo** _kohr_·toh/_loon_·goh
tight/loose	**stretto/largo** _streht_·toh/_lahr_·goh
Do you have this in size...?	**Non c'è la taglia...?** nohn cheh lah _tah_·llyah...
Do you have this in a bigger/smaller size?	**Non c'è in una taglia più grande/piccola?** nohn cheh een _oo_·nah _tah_·llyah pyoo _grahn_·deh/_peek_·koh·lah

For Numbers, see page 167.

Colors

I'd like something...	**Vorrei qualcosa di...**	*vohr•ray kwahl•koh•zah dee...*
beige	**beige**	*beyj*
black	**nero**	*neh•roh*
blue	**blu**	*bloo*
brown	**marrone**	*mahr•roh•neh*
green	**verde**	*vehr•deh*
gray	**grigio**	*gree•jyoh*
orange	**arancione**	*ahr•ahn•chyoh•neh*
pink	**rosa**	*roh•zah*
purple	**viola**	*vyoh•lah*
red	**rosso**	*rohs•soh*
white	**bianco**	*byahn•koh*
yellow	**giallo**	*jyahl•loh*

Clothes & Accessories

a backpack	**lo zaino**	*loh dzah•ee•noh*
a belt	**la cintura**	*lah cheen•too•rah*
a bikini	**il bikini**	*eel bee•kee•nee*
a blouse	**la camicia**	*lah kah•mee•chyah*
a bra	**il reggiseno**	*eel reh•djee•seh•noh*
briefs [underpants]/	**lo slip**	*loh sleep*
panties		
a coat	**il cappotto**	*eel kahp•poht•toh*
a dress	**il vestito da donna**	*eel veh•stee•toh dah dohn•nah*
a hat	**il cappello**	*eel kahp•pehl•loh*
a jacket	**la giacca**	*lah jyahk•kah*
jeans	**i jeans**	*ee jeenz*
pajamas	**il pigiama**	*eel pee•jyah•mah*
pants [trousers]	**i pantaloni**	*ee pahn•tah•loh•nee*
pantyhose [tights]	**il collant**	*eel kohl•lant*

a purse [handbag]	**la borsa** *lah bohr•sah*
a raincoat	**l'impermeabile** *leem•pehr•meh•ah•bee•leh*
a scarf	**la sciarpa** *lah shahr•pah*
a shirt	**la camicia** *lah kah•mee•chyah*
shorts	**i pantaloncini** *ee pahn•tah•lohn•chee•nee*
a skirt	**la gonna** *lah gohn•nah*
socks	**i calzini** *ee kahl•tsee•nee*
a suit	**l'abito** *lah•bee•toh*
sunglasses	**gli occhiali da sole** *llyee ohk•kyah•lee dah soh•leh*
a sweater	**il maglione** *eel mah•llyoh•neh*
a sweatshirt	**la felpa** *lah fehl•pah*
a swimsuit	**il costume da bagno** *eel koh•stoo•meh dah bah•nyoh*
a T-shirt	**la maglietta** *lah mah•llyeht•tah*
a tie	**la cravatta** *lah krah•vaht•tah*
underwear	**la biancheria intima** *lah byahn•keh•ree•ah een•tee•mah*

YOU MAY SEE...

UOMO	men's
DONNA	women's
BAMBINO	children's

Fabric

I'd like...	**Lo m /La f vorrei di...** loh/lah vohr·<u>ray</u> dee...
cotton	**cotone** koh·<u>toh</u>·neh
denim	**jeans** <u>jeenz</u>
lace	**pizzo** <u>pee</u>·tsoh
leather	**pelle** <u>pehl</u>·leh
linen	**lino** <u>lee</u>·noh
silk	**seta** <u>seh</u>·tah
wool	**lana** <u>lah</u>·nah
Is it machine washable?	**Si può lavare in lavatrice?** see pwoh lah·<u>vah</u>·reh een lah·vah·<u>tree</u>·cheh

Shoes

I'd like a pair of...	**Vorrei un paio di...** vohr·<u>ray</u> oon pah·<u>yoh</u> dee...
high-heels/flats	**scarpe col tacco alto/scarpe basse** skahr·peh kohl tahk·koh ahl·toh/skahr·peh bahs·seh
boots	**stivali** stee·<u>vah</u>·lee
loafers	**mocassini** moh·kahs·<u>see</u>·nee
sandals	**sandali** sahn·<u>dah</u>·lee
shoes	**scarpe** <u>skahr</u>·peh
slippers	**le ciabatte** leh chah·<u>baht</u>·teh
sneakers	**scarpe da tennis** <u>skahr</u>·peh dah tehn·<u>nees</u>
In size...	**Numero...** <u>noo</u>·meh·roh...

For Numbers, see page 167.

Sizes

small (S)	**piccola/S** <u>pee</u>·koh·lah/<u>ehs</u>·seh
medium (M)	**media/M** <u>meh</u>·dyah/<u>ehm</u>·meh
large (L)	**grande/L** <u>grahn</u>·deh/<u>ehl</u>·leh
extra large (XL)	**extra large/XL** <u>ehk</u>·strah lahrj/<u>ehks</u>·ehl
petite	**piccola** peehk·koh·lah
plus size	**taglia forte** <u>tah</u>·llyah <u>fohr</u>·teh

Newsstand & Tobacconist

Do you sell English-language newspapers?	**Avete qualche giornale in inglese?** *ah·veh·teh kwahl·keh jyohr·nah·leh een een·gleh·zeh*
I'd like...	**Vorrei...** *vohr·ray...*
candy [sweets]	**delle caramelle** *dehl·leh kah·rah·mehl·leh*
chewing gum	**della gomma da masticare** *dehl·lah gohm·mah dah mah·stee·kah·reh*
a chocolate bar	**del cioccolato** *dehl chyohk·koh·lah·toh*
a cigar	**un sigaro** *oon see·gah·roh*
a pack/carton of cigarettes	**un pacchetto/una stecca di sigarette** *oon pahk·keht·toh/oo·nah stehk·kah dee see·gah·reht·teh*
a lighter	**un accendino** *oon·ah·chehn·dee·noh*
a magazine	**una rivista** *oo·nah ree·vee·stah*
matches	**dei fiammiferi** *day fyahm·mee·feh·ree*
a newspaper	**un giornale** *oon jyohr·nah·leh*
a pen	**una penna** *oo·nah pehn·nah*
a postcard	**una cartolina** *oo·nah kahr·toh·lee·nah*
a (road)/town map of...	**una cartina (stradale) di...** *oo·nah kahr·tee·nah (strah·dah·lee) dee...*
stamps	**dei francobolli** *day frahn·koh·bohl·lee*

Photography

I'd like a/an... camera.	**Vorrei una macchina fotografica...** *vohr·ray oo·nah mahk·kee·nah foh·toh·grah·fee·kah...*
automatic	**automatica** *ow·toh·mah·tee·kah*
digital	**digitale** *dee·jee·tah·leh*
disposable	**usa e getta** *oo·zah eh jeht·tah*
I'd like...	**Vorrei...** *vohr·ray...*
digital prints	**far stampare delle foto digitali** *fahr stahm·pah·reh dehl·leh foh·toh dee·jee·tah·lee*

English-language newspapers, magazines and books can usually be found at newsstands, especially at train stations and in airports.
Smoking is not allowed in any public facility (banks, offices, bars, cafes, restaurants, buses, trains, etc.). Be aware that 'No Smoking' signs are not posted but you will incur a high fine if caught smoking in any public indoor area.

a battery	**una batteria** _oo•nah baht•teh•ree•ah_
a memory card	**una scheda memoria** _oo•nah skeh•dah meh•moh•ryah_
Can I print digital photos here?	**Posso stampare foto digitali?** _pohs•soh stahm•pah•reh foh•toh dee•jee•tah•lee_

Souvenirs

blown glass	**il vetro soffiato** _eel veh•troh sohf•fyah•toh_
bottle of wine	**la bottiglia di vino** _lah boht•tee•llyah dee vee•noh_
box of chocolates	**la scatola di cioccolatini** _lah skah•toh•lah dee chyohk•koh•lah•tee•nee_
wood carvings	**il legno intagliato** _eel leh•nyoh een•tah•llyah•toh_
crystal	**il cristallo** _eel kree•stahl•loh_
doll	**la bambola** _lah bahm•boh•lah_
key ring	**il portachiavi** _eel pohr•tah•kyah•vee_
lace	**il pizzo** _eel pee•tsoh_
postcard	**la cartolina** _lah kahr•toh•lee•nah_
pottery	**la ceramica** _lah cheh•rah•mee•kah_
T-shirt	**la maglietta** _lah mah•llyeht•tah_
toy	**il giocattolo** _eel jyoh•kaht•toh•loh_
Can I see…?	**Posso vedere…?** _pohs•soh veh•deh•reh…_
Is this real?	**È vero?** _eh veh•roh_

It's in the window/ display case.	**È in vetrina/nella vetrinetta.** *eh een veh·tree·nah/ nehl·lah veh·tree·neht·tah*
I'd like…	**Vorrei…** *vohr·ray…*
a battery	**una batteria** *oo·nah baht·teh·ree·ah*
a bracelet	**un braccialetto** *oon brah·chyah·leht·toh*
a brooch	**una spilla** *oo·nah speel·lah*
a clock	**un orologio** *oo·noh·roh·loh·jyoh*
earrings	**un paio di orecchini** *oon pah·yoh dee oh·rehk·kee·ne*
a necklace	**una collana** *oo·nah kohl·lah·nah*
a ring	**un anello** *oo·nah·nehl·loh*
a watch	**un orologio** *oo·noh·roh·loh·jyoh*
I'd like…	**Lo *m*/La *f* vorrei…** *loh/lah vohr·ray…*
copper	**di rame** *dee rah·meh*
crystal	**in cristallo** *een kree·stahl·loh*
diamonds	**di diamanti** *dee dyah·mahn·tee*
white/yellow gold	**d'oro bianco/giallo** *doh·roh byahn·koh/jyahl·loh*
pearls	**di perle** *dee pehr·leh*
pewter	**di peltro** *dee pehl·troh*
platinum	**di platino** *dee plah·tee·noh*
sterling silver	**d'argento** *dahr·jehn·toh*
Can you engrave it?	**Potete fare un'incisione?** *poh·teh·teh fah·reh oo·neen·chee·zyoh·neh*

Italy offers an endless variety of handicrafts, from mouth-blown Murano glassware and delicate Capodimonte porcelain creations, to world-renowned fashion, antiques and of course gastronomic specialties. Traditional souvenirs are usually more expensive at souvenir shops. Local markets and small shops are also great places to find unique souvenirs.

Sport & Leisure

ESSENTIAL

When's the game?	**A che ora c'è la partita?** *ah keh <u>oh</u>•rah cheh lah pahr•<u>tee</u>•tah*
Where's…?	**Dov'è…?** *doh•<u>veh</u>…*
the beach	**la spiaggia** *lah <u>spyah</u>•djah*
the park	**il parco** *eel <u>pahr</u>•koh*
the pool	**la piscina** *lah pee•<u>shee</u>•nah*
Is it safe to swim here?	**Si può nuotare?** *see pwoh nwoh•<u>tah</u>•reh*
Can I hire golf clubs?	**Posso noleggiare delle mazze?** *<u>pohs</u>•soh noh•leh•<u>djah</u>•reh <u>dehl</u>•leh <u>mah</u>•tseh*
How much per hour?	**Qual è la tariffa per un'ora?** *<u>kwah</u>•leh lah tah•<u>reef</u>•fah pehr oo•<u>noh</u>•rah*
How far is it to…?	**Quanto dista a…?** *<u>kwahn</u>•toh <u>dee</u>•stah ah…*
Can you show me on the map?	**Può indicarmelo sulla cartina?** *pwoh een•dee•<u>kahr</u>•meh•loh <u>sool</u>•lah kahr•<u>tee</u>•nah*

Il calcio (soccer) is Italy's most popular year-round sport. Skiing and snowboarding are favorite winter pastimes for Italians. During the summer, sailing, windsurfing, hiking, tennis, scuba-diving, hang-gliding—especially on Lake Garda—and swimming are enjoyed.

Watching Sport

When's...?	**A che ora c'è...?** ah keh <u>oh</u>•rah cheh...
the baseball game	**la partita di baseball** lah pahr•<u>tee</u>•tah dee <u>bays</u>•bahl
the basketball game	**la partita di basket** lah pahr•<u>tee</u>•tah dee <u>bahs</u>•keht
the boxing match	**l'incontro di boxe** leen•<u>kohn</u>•troh dee <u>boh</u>•kseh
the cricket game	**partita di cricket** pahr•tee•tah dee kree•keht
the cycling race	**la gara di ciclismo** lah <u>gah</u>•rah dee chee•<u>kleez</u>•moh
the golf game	**la partita di golf** lah pahr•<u>tee</u>•tah dee gohlf
the soccer [football] game	**la partita di calcio** lah pahr•<u>tee</u>•tah dee <u>kahl</u>•chyoh
the tennis match	**la partita di tennis** lah pahr•<u>tee</u>•tah dee <u>tehn</u>•nees
the volleyball game	**la partita di pallavolo** lah pahr•<u>tee</u>•tah dee pahl•lah•<u>voh</u>•loh
Who's playing?	**Chi gioca?** kee <u>jyoh</u>•kah
Where's the racetrack/stadium?	**Dov'è il circuito/lo stadio?** doh•<u>veh</u> eel cheer•<u>kwee</u>•toh/loh <u>stah</u>•dyoh
Where can I place a bet?	**Dove si fanno le scommesse?** <u>doh</u>•veh see <u>fahn</u>•noh leh skohm•<u>mehs</u>•seh

For Tickets, see page 19.

Playing Sport

Where is/Where are...?	**Dov'è/Dove sono...?** doh-_veh_/_doh_-veh soh-noh...
the golf course	**il campo da golf** eel _kahm_-poh dah gohlf
the gym	**la palestra** lah pah-_leh_-strah
the park	**il parco** eel _pahr_-koh
the tennis courts	**i campi da tennis** ee _kahm_-pee dah _teh_-nees
How much...?	**Quant'è la tariffa per...?** kwahn-_teh_ lah tah-_reef_-fah pehr...
per day	**un giorno** oon _jyohr_-noh
per hour	**un'ora** oon-_oh_-rah
per game	**una partita** _oo_-nah pahr-_tee_-tah
per round	**un turno/round?** oon toohr-noh/oon rah-uh-nd?
Can I hire...	**Posso noleggiare...** _pohs_-soh noh-leh-_djah_-reh...
some golf clubs	**delle mazze** _dehl_-leh _mah_-tseh
some equipment	**l'attrezzatura** laht-treh-tsah-_too_-rah
a racket	**una racchetta** _oo_-nah rahk-_keht_-tah

At the Beach/Pool

Where's the beach/pool?	**Dov'è la spiaggia/piscina?** doh-_veh_ lah _spyah_-djah/pee-_shee_-nah
Is there...?	**C'è...?** cheh...
a kiddie pool	**una piscina per bambini** _oo_-nah pee-_shee_-nah pehr bahm-_bee_-nee
a indoor/outdoor pool	**una piscina interna/esterna** _oo_-nah pee-_shee_-nah een-_tehr_-nah/eh-_stehr_-nah
a lifeguard	**il bagnino** eel bah-_nyee_-noh
Is it safe to swim/dive?	**Si può nuotare/tuffarsi?** see pwoh nwoh-_tah_-reh/toof-_fahr_-see
Is it safe for children?	**È per bambini?** eh pehr bahm-_bee_-nee
I'd like to hire...	**Vorrei noleggiare...** vohr-_ray_ noh-leh-_djah_-reh

a deck chair	**una sedia a sdraio** _oo_•nah _seh_•dyah ah _sdrah_•yoh
a jet ski	**un acquascooter** oon _ah_•kwah•_skoo_•tehr
diving equipment	**l'attrezzatura subacquea** laht•treh•tsah•_too_•rah soo•_bah_•kweh•ah
a motorboat	**un motoscafo** oon moh•toh•_skah_•foh
a rowboat	**una barca a remi** _oo_•nah _bahr_•kah ah _reh_•mee
snorkeling equipment	**una maschera e il boccaglio** _oo_•nah _mah_•skeh•rah eh eel bohk•_kah_•llyoh
a surfboard	**una tavola da surf** _oo_•nah _tah_•voh•lah dah soorf
a towel	**un asciugamano** oon ah•shyoo•gah•_mah_•noh
an umbrella	**un ombrellone** oon ohm•brehl•_loh_•neh
water skis	**sci nautici** shee _now_•tee•chee
a windsurfer	**un windsurf** oon _weend_•soorf
For…hours.	**Per…ore.** pehr…_oh_•reh

With 7,600 kilometers (4,722 miles) of coastline, Italy has beaches to suit all tastes and budgets. From exclusive Ligurian and Sardinian beaches to popular Versilian and Adriatic spots, the seaside is a favorite holiday destination for Italians. Privately managed beaches are usually well-kept and offer a variety of services for a daily fee.

YOU MAY SEE...

SKI LIFT	drag lift
FUNIVIA	cable car
SEGGIOVIA	chair lift
PRINCIPIANTE	novice
INTERMEDIO	intermediate
ESPERTO	expert
PISTA CHIUSA	trail [piste] closed

Winter Sports

A lift pass for a day/ five days, please	**Un lift pass per un giorno/cinque giorni, per favore.** *oon leeft pahs pehr oon jyohr·noh/ cheen·kweh jyohr·nee pehr fah·voh·reh*
I'd like to hire...	**Vorrei noleggiare...** *vohr·ray noh·leh·djah·reh...*
boots	**un paio di stivali** *oon pah·yoh dee stee·vah·lee*
a helmet	**un casco** *oon kah·skoh*
skis	**un paio di sci** *oon pah·yoh dee shee*
poles	**un paio di racchette da sci** *oon pah·yoh dee rahk·keht·teh dah shee*
a snowboard	**uno snowboard** *oo·noh snoh·bohrd*
snowshoes	**le scarpe da neve** *lah skahr·peh dah neh·veh*
These are too big/small.	**Sono troppo grandi/piccoli.** *soh·noh trohp·poh grahn·dee/peek·koh·lee*
Are there lessons?	**Si possono prendere lezioni?** *see pohs·soh·noh prehn·deh·reh leh·tsyoh·nee*
I'm a beginner.	**Sono principiante.** *soh·noh preen·chee·pyahn·teh*
I'm experienced.	**Sono esperto m /esperta f.** *soh·noh eh·spehr·toh/ eh·spehr·tah*
A trail [piste] map, please.	**Una cartina delle piste, per favore.** *oo·nah kahr·tee·nah dehl·leh pee·steh pehr fah·voh·reh*

Out in the Country

A map…, please.	**Una cartina…, per favore.** <u>oo</u>•nah kahr•<u>tee</u>•nah… pehr fah•<u>voh</u>•reh
of this region	**della regione** <u>dehl</u>•lah reh•<u>jyoh</u>•neh
of the walking routes	**dei sentieri pedonali** day sehn•<u>tyeh</u>•ree peh•doh•<u>nah</u>•lee
of the bike routes	**delle piste ciclabili** <u>dehl</u>•leh <u>pee</u>•steh chee•<u>klah</u>•bee•lee
of the trails	**dei sentieri** day sehn•<u>tyeh</u>•ree
Is it…?	**È…?** eh…
easy	**facile** <u>fah</u>•chee•leh
difficult	**difficile** deef•<u>fee</u>•chee•leh
far	**lontano** lohn•<u>tah</u>•noh
steep	**ripido** <u>ree</u>•pee•doh
How far is it to…?	**Quanto dista a…?** <u>kwahn</u>•toh <u>dee</u>•stah ah…
Can you show me on the map?	**Può indicarmelo sulla cartina?** pwoh een•dee•<u>kahr</u>•meh•loh <u>sool</u>•lah kahr•<u>tee</u>•nah
I'm lost.	**Mi sono perso m /persa f.** mee <u>soh</u>•noh <u>pehr</u>•soh/<u>pehr</u>•sah
Where's…?	**Dov'è…?** doh•<u>veh</u>…
the bridge	**il ponte** eel <u>pohn</u>•teh
the cave	**la grotta** lah <u>groht</u>•tah
the desert	**il deserto?** eel deh•<u>sehr</u>•toh?
the farm	**la fattoria** lah faht•toh•<u>ree</u>•ah
the field	**il campo** eel <u>kahm</u>•poh
the forest	**la foresta** lah foh•<u>reh</u>•stah
the hill	**la collina** lah kohl•<u>lee</u>•nah
the lake	**il lago** eel <u>lah</u>•goh
the mountain	**la montagna** lah mohn•<u>tah</u>•nyah
the nature preserve	**la riserva naturale** lah ree•<u>sehr</u>•vah nah•too•<u>rah</u>•leh
the viewpoint	**il belvedere** eel behl•veh•<u>deh</u>•reh
the park	**il parco** eel <u>pahr</u>•koh

the path	**il sentiero** *eel sehn·tyeh·roh*	
the peak	**il picco** *eel peek·koh*	
the picnic area	**l'area picnic** *lah·reh·ah peek·neek*	
the pond	**lo stagno** *loh stah·nyoh*	
the river	**il fiume** *eel fyoo·meh*	
the sea	**il mare** *eel mah·reh*	
the (thermal) spring	**la sorgente (termale)** *lah sohr·jehn·teh (tehr·mah·leh)*	
the stream	**il ruscello** *eel roo·shehl·loh*	
the valley	**la valle** *lah vahl·leh*	
the vineyard	**il vigneto** *eel vee·nyeh·toh*	
the waterfall	**la cascata** *lah kah·skah·tah*	

Going Out

ESSENTIAL

What's there to do at night?	**Cosa si fa di sera?** *koh·zah see fah dee seh·rah*
Do you have a program of events?	**Mi può dare un calendario degli eventi?** *mee pwoh dah·reh oon kah·lehn·dah·ryoh deh·llyee eh·vehn·tee*
What's playing tonight?	**Cosa c'è in programma stasera?** *koh·zah cheh een proh·grahm·mah stah·seh·rah*
Where's...?	**Dov'è...?** *doh·veh...*
the downtown area	**il centro** *eel chehn·troh*
the bar	**il bar** *eel bahr*
the dance club	**la discoteca** *lah dee·skoh·teh·kah*
Is there a cover charge?	**C'è un costo aggiuntivo?** *cheh oon koh·stoh ah·djoon·tee·voh*

Entertainment

Can you recommend...?	**Può consigliarmi...?** *pwoh kohn•see•llyahr•mee...*
a concert	**un concerto** *oon kohn•chehr•toh*
a movie	**un film** *oon feelm*
an opera	**un'opera** *oo•noh•peh•rah*
a play	**una rappresentazione teatrale** *oo•nah rahp•preh•zehn•tah•tsyoh•neh teh•ah•trah•leh*
When does it start/end?	**Quando inizia/finisce?** *kwahn•doh ee•nee•tsyah/fee•nee•sheh*
What's the dress code?	**Come ci si deve vestire?** *koh•meh chee see deh•veh veh•stee•reh*
I like...	**Mi piace...** *mee pyah•cheh...*
classical music	**la musica classica** *lah moo•zee•kah klah•see•kah*
folk music	**la musica folk** *lah moo•zee•kah fohlk*

YOU MAY HEAR...

Spegnere il cellulare, per favore. *speh•nyeh•reh eel chehl•loo•lah•reh pehr fah•voh•reh* Turn off your cell [mobile] phones, please.

A calendar of events may be found at local tourist information offices or on the venues' websites. Local events are often posted around town, so be sure to stop and read the posters. The hotel concierge is also a good source for local information.

jazz	**il jazz** *eel jahz*
pop music	**la musica pop** *lah moo·zee·kah pohp*
rap	**il rap** *eel rahp*

For Tickets, see page 19.

Nightlife

What's there to do at night?	**Cosa si fa di sera?** *koh·zah see fah dee seh·rah*
Can you recommend...?	**Può consigliarmi...?** *pwoh kohn·see·llyahr·mee...*
a bar	**un bar** *oon bahr*
a casino	**un casinò** *oon kah·zee·noh*
a dance club	**una discoteca** *oo·nah dee·skoh·teh·kah*
a gay club	**un locale gay** *oon loh·kah·leh gay*
a jazz club	**un locale jazz** *oon loh·kah·leh jahz*
a club with Italian music	**un locale con musica italiana** *oon loh·kah·leh kohn moo·zee·kah ee·tah·lyah·nah*
Is there live music?	**C'è musica dal vivo?** *cheh moo·zee·kah dahl vee·voh*
How do I get there?	**Come ci si arriva?** *koh·meh chee see ahr·ree·vah*
Is there a cover charge?	**C'è un costo aggiuntivo?** *cheh oon koh·stoh ah·djoon·tee·voh*
Let's go dancing.	**Andiamo a ballare.** *ahn·dyah·moh ah bahl·lah·reh*
Is this area safe at night?	**Questa zona è sicura di notte?** *Kweh·stah·dzoh·nah eh see·koo·rah dee noht·teh?*

Special Requirements

Business Travel   14
Traveling with Children   14
Disabled Travelers   14

Business Travel

ESSENTIAL

I'm here on business.	**Sono qui per lavoro.** <u>soh</u>•noh kwee pehr lah•<u>voh</u>•roh
Here's my business card.	**Ecco il mio biglietto da visita.** <u>ehk</u>•koh eel <u>mee</u>•oh bee•<u>llyeht</u>•toh dah <u>vee</u>•zee•tah
Can I have your card?	**Mi può dare il suo biglietto da visita?** mee pwoh <u>dah</u>•reh eel <u>soo</u>•oh bee•<u>llyeht</u>•toh dah <u>vee</u>•zee•tah
I have a meeting with…	**Ho una riunione con…** oh <u>oo</u>•nah ryoo•<u>nyoh</u>•neh kohn…
Where's…?	**Dov'è…?** doh•<u>veh</u>…
the business center	**il centro business** eel <u>chehn</u>•troh <u>bees</u>•nehs
the convention hall	**la sala congressi** lah <u>sah</u>•lah kohn•<u>grehs</u>•see
the meeting room	**la sala meeting** lah <u>sah</u>•lah <u>mee</u>•teeng

Buongiorno (good morning) or **buonasera** (good afternoon/evening) are suitable greetings in business situations, and are often accompanied by a handshake. **Piacere** (pleased to meet you) is a polite response at introductions. When saying goodbye to business acquaintances, it is polite to use the formal **arrivederla**.

On Business

I'm here for…	**Sono qui per…** <u>soh</u>•noh kwee pehr…
a seminar	**un seminario** oon seh•mee•<u>nah</u>•ryoh
a conference	**una conferenza** <u>oo</u>•nah kohn•feh•<u>rehn</u>•tsah
a meeting	**una riunione** <u>oo</u>•nah ryoo•<u>nyoh</u>•neh

My name is…	**Mi chiamo…** *mee kyah•moh…*
May I introduce my colleague…	**Le presento il mio collega *m* /la mia collega *f*…** *leh preh•zehn•toh eel mee•oh kohl•leh•gah/ lah mee•ah kohl•leh•gah…*
I have a meeting/ an appointment with…	**Ho una riunione/un appuntamento con…** *oh oo•nah ryoo•nyoh•neh/oon ahp•poon•tah•mehn•toh kohn…*
I'm sorry I'm late.	**Scusi il ritardo.** *skoo•see eel ree•tahr•doh*
I need an interpreter.	**Mi serve un interprete.** *mee sehr•veh oon een•tehr•preh•teh*
You can contact me at the…Hotel.	**Sono raggiungibile all'hotel…** *soh•noh rah•djoon•jee•bee•leh ahl•loh•tehl…*

YOU MAY HEAR…

Ha un appuntamento? *ah oon ahp•poon•tah•mehn•toh*	Do you have an appointment?
Con chi? *kohn kee*	With whom?
Il signor *m* /La signora *f* è in riunione. *eel see•nyohr/lah see•nyoh•rah eh een ryoo•nyoh•neh*	He/She is in a meeting.
Un momento, per favore. *oon moh•mehn•toh pehr fah•voh•reh*	One moment, please.
Si accomodi. *see ahk•koh•moh•dee*	Have a seat.
Desidera qualcosa da bere? *deh•zee•deh•rah kwahl•koh•zah dah beh•reh*	Would you like something to drink?
Grazie per essere venuto *m* /venuta *f*. *grah•tsyeh pehr eh•seh•reh veh•noo•toh/ veh•noo•tah*	Thank you for coming.

I'm here until…	**Sono qui fino a…** _soh•noh kwee fee•noh ah…_
I need to…	**Ho bisogno di…** _oh bee•soh•nyoh dee…_
make a call	**fare una telefonata** _fah•reh oo•nah teh•leh•foh•nah•tah_
make a photocopy	**fare una fotocopia** _fah•reh oo•nah foh•toh•koh•pyah_
send an e-mail	**inviare un'e-mail** _een•vyah•reh oon ee•mayl_
send a fax	**inviare un fax** _een•vyah•reh oon fahks_
send a package (for next-day delivery)	**inviare un pacco (da un giorno all'altro)** _een•vyah•reh oon pahk•koh (dah oon jyohr•noh ahl•lahl•troh)_
It was a pleasure to meet you.	**È stato un piacere.** _eh stah•toh oon pyah•cheh•reh_

For Communications, see page 47.

Traveling with Children

ESSENTIAL

Is there a discount for kids?	**È previsto uno sconto per bambini?** _eh preh•vee•stoh oo•noh skohn•toh pehr bahm•bee•nee_
Can you recommend a babysitter?	**Può consigliarmi una babysitter?** _pwoh kohn•see•llyahr•mee oo•nah bah•bee•seet•tehr_
Do you have a child's seat/highchair?	**Avete un seggiolino/seggiolone per bambini?** _ah•veh•teh oon seh•djoh•lee•noh/seh•djoh•loh•neh pehr bahm•bee•nee_
Where can I change the baby?	**Dove posso cambiare il bambino?** _doh•veh poh•soh kahm•byah•reh eel bahm•bee•noh_

Out & About

Can you recommend something for kids?	**Può consigliarmi qualcosa per i bambini?** *pwoh kohn·see·llyahr·mee kwahl·koh·zah pehr ee bahm·bee·nee*
Where's…?	**Dov'è…?** *doh·veh…*
the amusement park	**il luna park** *eel loo·nah pahrk*
the arcade	**il parco videogiochi** *eel pahr·koh vee·deh·oh·jyoh·kee*
the kiddie [paddling] pool	**la piscina per bambini** *lah pee·shee·nah pehr bahm·bee·nee*
the park	**il parco** *eel pahr·koh*
the playground	**il parco giochi** *eel pahr·koh jyoh·kee*
the zoo	**lo zoo** *loh dzooh*
Are kids allowed?	**Si possono portare i bambini?** *see pohs·soh·noh pohr·tah·reh ee bahm·bee·nee*
Is it safe for kids?	**È per bambini?** *eh pehr bahm·bee·nee*
Is it suitable for… year olds?	**È adatto ai bambini di…anni?** *eh ah·daht·toh ah·ee bahm·bee·nee dee…ahn·nee*

For Numbers, see page 167.

YOU MAY HEAR…

Che carino m/carina f!
keh kah-<u>ree</u>-noh/kah-<u>ree</u>-nah

How cute!

Come si chiama? <u>koh</u>-meh see <u>kyah</u>-mah

What's his/her name?

Quanti anni ha? <u>kwahn</u>-tee <u>ahn</u>-nee ah

How old is he/she?

Baby Essentials

Do you have…?	**Avete…?** ah-<u>veh</u>-teh…
a baby bottle	**un biberon** oon bee-beh-<u>rohn</u>
baby food	**del cibo per neonati** dehl <u>chee</u>-boh pehr neh-oh-<u>nah</u>-tee
baby wipes	**delle salviette per neonati** <u>dehl</u>-leh sahl-<u>vyeht</u>-teh pehr neh-oh-<u>nah</u>-tee
a car seat	**un seggiolino per auto** oon seh-djoh-<u>lee</u>-noh pehr <u>ow</u>-toh
a children's menu/portion	**il menù/le porzioni per bambini** eel meh-<u>noo</u>/leh pohr-<u>tsyoh</u>-nee pehr bahm-<u>bee</u>-nee
a child's seat/highchair	**un seggiolino/seggiolone per bambini** oon seh-djoh-<u>lee</u>-noh/seh-djoh-<u>loh</u>-neh pehr bahm-<u>bee</u>-nee
a crib/cot	**una culla/un lettino** <u>oo</u>-nah <u>kool</u>-lah/oon leht-<u>tee</u>-noh
diapers [nappies]	**dei pannolini** day pahn-noh-<u>lee</u>-nee
formula [baby food]	**del latte in polvere** dehl <u>laht</u>-teh een <u>pohl</u>-veh-reh
a pacifier [dummy]	**un ciucciotto** oon chyoo-<u>chyoht</u>-toh
a playpen	**un box** oon bohks
a stroller [pushchair]	**un passeggino** oon pah-seh-<u>djee</u>-noh

| Can I breastfeed the baby here? | **Posso allattare il bambino?** _poh_•soh _ahl•laht•tah•reh eel bahm•bee•noh_ |
| Where can I breastfeed/change the baby? | **Dove posso allattare/cambiare il bambino?** _doh_•veh _poh_•soh _ahl•laht•tah•reh/ kahm•byah•reh eel bahm•bee•noh_ |

For Dining with Children, see page 63.

Babysitting

Can you recommend a babysitter?	**Può consigliarmi una babysitter?** _pwoh kohn•see•llyahr•mee oo•nah bah•bee•seet•tehr_
What do you/they charge?	**Quanto si paga?** _kwahn•toh see pah•gah_
I'll be back at...	**Torno per le...** _tohr•noh pehr leh..._
If you need to contact me, call...	**Mi potete trovare al numero...** _mee poh•tay•teh troh•vahr•eh ahl noo•meh•roh..._

For Numbers, see page 167.

For Time, see page 169.

Health & Emergency

| Can you recommend a pediatrician? | **Può consigliarmi un pediatra?** _pwoh kohn•see•llyahr•mee oon peh•dyah•trah_ |

My son/daughter is allergic to…	**Il mio bambino/La mia bambina è allergico m / allergica f a…** *eel mee•oh bahm•bee•noh/lah mee•ah bahm•bee•nah eh ahl•lehr•jee•koh/ahl•lehr•jee•kah ah…*
My son/daughter is missing.	**Il mio bambino m /La mia bambina f è scomparso m /scomparsa f.** *eel mee•oh bahm•bee•noh/lah mee•ah bahm•bee•nah eh skohm•pahr•soh/skohm•pahr•sah*
Have you seen a boy/girl?	**Ha visto un bambino m /una bambina f?** *ah vee•stoh oon bahm•bee•noh/oo•nah bahm•bee•nah*

For Meals & Cooking, see page 65.

For Health, see page 153.

For Police, see page 151.

Disabled Travelers

ESSENTIAL

Is there…?	**C'è…?** *cheh…*
access for the disabled	**l'accesso ai disabili** *lah•cheh•soh ah•ee dee•zah•bee•lee*
a wheelchair ramp	**la rampa per le sedie a rotelle** *lah rahm•pah pehr leh seh•dyeh ah roh•tehl•leh*
a disabled-accessible toilet	**la toilette per i disabili** *lah twah•leht pehr ee dee•zah•bee•lee*
I need…	**Mi serve…** *mee sehr•veh…*
assistance	**assistenza** *ah•see•stehn•tsah*
an elevator [a lift]	**un ascensore** *oon ah•shehn•soh•reh*
a ground-floor room	**una stanza al pianterreno** *oo•nah stahn•tsah ahl pyahn•tehr•reh•noh*

Asking for Assistance

I'm...	**Sono...** _soh_•noh...
disabled	**disabile** dee•_zah_•bee•leh
visually impaired	**ipovedente** ee•poh•veh•_dehn_•the
deaf	**sordo** sohr-doh
hearing impaired	**audioleso** ow•dyoh•_leh_•soh
I cannot walk far/ use the stairs.	**Non posso camminare tanto/fare le scale.** nohn _poh_•soh kahm•mee•_nah_•reh _tahn_•toh/ _fah_•reh leh _skah_•leh
Can I bring my wheelchair?	**Posso portare la sedia a rotelle?** _poh_•soh pohr•_tah_•reh lah _seh_•dyah ah roh•_tehl_•leh
Are guide dogs permitted?	**I cani guida sono permessi?** ee _kah_•nee _gwee_•dah _soh_•noh pehr•_meh_•see
Can you help me?	**Può aiutarmi?** pwoh ah•yoo•_tahr_•mee
Please open/hold the door.	**Per favore, potrebbe aprire/tenere aperta la porta.** pehr fah•_voh_•reh poh•_trehb_•beh ah•_pree_•reh/ teh•_neh_•reh ah•_pehr_•tah lah _pohr_•tah

In an Emergency

Emergencies	150
Police	151
Health	153
The Basics	162

Emergencies

ESSENTIAL

Help!	**Aiuto!** *ah•yoo•toh*
Go away!	**Se ne vada!** *seh neh vah•dah*
Stop, thief!	**Fermi, al ladro!** *fehr•mee ahl lah•droh*
Get a doctor!	**Un medico!** *oon meh•dee•koh*
Fire!	**Al fuoco!** *ahl fwoh•koh*
I'm lost.	**Mi sono perso *m* /persa *f*.** *mee soh•noh pehr•soh/pehr•sah*
Can you help me?	**Può aiutarmi?** *pwoh ah•yoo•tahr•mee*

In an emergency, dial: **112** for the police
115 for the fire brigade
118 for the ambulance.

YOU MAY HEAR...

Riempia questo modulo. *ree•ehm•pyah kweh•stoh moh•doo•loh*

Fill out this form.

Un documento, per favore. *oon doh•koo•mehn•toh pehr fah•voh•reh*

Your identification, please.

Quando/Dove è successo? *kwahn•doh/doh•veh eh soo•cheh•soh*

When/Where did it happen?

Che aspetto aveva? *keh ah•speht•toh ah•veh•vah*

What does he/she look like?

150

Police

ESSENTIAL

Call the police!	**Chiami la polizia!** _kyah·mee lah poh·lee·tsee·ah_
Where's the police station?	**Dov'è il commissariato?** _doh·veh eel kohm·mee·sah·ryah·toh_
There was an accident/attack.	**C'è stato un incidente/stata un'aggressione.** _cheh stah·toh oon een·chee·dehn·teh/stah·tah oo·nahg·grehs·syoh·neh_
My son/daughter is missing.	**Il mio bambino _m_ /La mia bambina _f_ è scomparso _m_ /scomparsa _f_.** _eel mee·oh bahm·bee·noh/lah mee·ah bahm·bee·nah eh skohm·pahr·soh/skohm·pahr·sah_
I need an interpreter	**Ho bisogno di un interprete.** _oh bee·soh·nyoh dee oon een·tehr·preh·teh_
I'm innocent.	**Sono innocente.** _soh·noh een·noh·chehn·teh_
I need to contact my lawyer/make a phone call.	**Ho bisogno di chiamare il mio avvocato/fare una telefonata.** _oh bee·soh·nyoh dee kyah·mah·reh eel mee·oh ahv·voh·kah·toh/fah·reh oo·nah teh·leh·foh·nah·tah_

Crime & Lost Property

I want to report...	**Vorrei denunciare...** _vohr·ray deh·noon·chyah·reh..._
a mugging	**uno scippo** _oo·noh sheep·poh_
a rape	**uno stupro** _oo·noh stoo·proh_
a theft	**un furto** _oon foor·toh_
I've been mugged/robbed.	**Mi hanno scippato/derubato.** _mee ahn·noh sheep·pah·toh/deh·roo·bah·toh_
I've lost my...	**Ho perso...** _oh pehr·soh..._

My…was stolen.	**Mi hanno rubato…** *mee ahn·noh roo·bah·toh*
backpack	**lo zaino** *loh dzah·ee·noh*
bicycle	**la bicicletta** *lah bee·chee·kleht·tah*
camera	**la macchina fotografica** *lah mahk·kee·nah foh·toh·grah·fee·kah*
computer	**il computer** *eel kohm·pyoo·tehr*
(hire) car	**l'auto a noleggio** *l·ow·toh ah noh·leh·djoh*
credit card	**la carta di credito** *lah kahr·tah dee kreh·dee·toh*
jewelry	**i gioielli** *ee joy·ehl·lee*
money	**il denaro** *eel deh·nah·roh*
passport	**il passaporto** *eel pahs·sah·pohr·toh*
purse [handbag]	**la borsa** *lah bohr·sah*
traveler's checks [cheques]	**i travelers cheques** *ee trah·vehl·lehrs chehks*
wallet	**il portafogli** *eel pohr·tah·foh·llyee*
I need a police report.	**Ho bisogno di un verbale.** *oh bee·soh·nyoh dee oon vehr·bah·leh*
Where is the British/American/Irish embassy?	**Dove si trova l'ambasciata britannica/americana/irlandese?** *Doh·veh see troh·vah l·ahm·bah·shah·tah bree·tahn·nee·kah/ah·meh·ree·kah·nah/eer·lahn·deh·seh.*

Health

ESSENTIAL

I'm sick [ill].	**Sto male.** *stoh mah·leh*
I need an English-speaking doctor.	**Ho bisogno di un medico che parli inglese.** *oh bee·soh·nyoh dee oon meh·dee·koh keh pahr·lee een·gleh·zeh*
It hurts here.	**Mi fa male qui.** *mee fah mah·leh kwee*
I have a stomachache.	**Ho mal di stomaco.** *oh mahl dee stoh·mah·koh*

Finding a Doctor

Can you recommend a doctor/dentist?	**Mi può consigliare un medico/dentista?** *mee pwoo kohn·see·llyah·reh oon meh·dee·koh/ dehn·tee·stah*
Can the doctor come here?	**Il medico può venire?** *eel meh·dee·koh pwoh veh·nee·reh*
I need an English-speaking doctor.	**Ho bisogno di un medico che parli inglese.** *oh bee·soh·nyoh dee oon meh·dee·koh keh pahr·lee een·gleh·zeh*
What are the office hours?	**Che orari fate?** *keh oh·rah·ree fah·teh*
I'd like an appointment for...	**Vorrei un appuntamento...** *vohr·ray oon ahp·poon·tah·mehn·toh...*
today	**per oggi** *pehr oh·djee*
tomorrow	**per domani** *pehr doh·mah·nee*
as soon as possible	**al più presto possibile** *ahl pyoo preh·stoh pohs·see·bee·leh*
It's urgent.	**È urgente.** *eh oor·jehn·teh*

Symptoms

I'm bleeding.	**Perdo sangue.** _pehr_·doh _sahn_·gweh	
I'm constipated.	**Sono costipato.** _soh_·noh koh·stee·_pah_·toh	
I'm dizzy.	**Mi gira la testa.** mee _jee_·rah lah _teh_·stah	
I'm nauseous.	**Ho la nausea.** oh lah _now_·zeh·ah	
I'm vomiting.	**Vomito.** _voh_·mee·toh	
It hurts here.	**Mi fa male qui.** mee fah _mah_·leh kwee	
I have...	**Ho...** oh...	
an allergic reaction	**una reazione allergica** _oo_·nah reh·ah·_tsyoh_·neh ahl·_lehr_·jee·kah	
chest pain	**un dolore al petto** oon doh·_loh_·reh ahl _peht_·toh	
cramps	**crampi** krahm·pee	
diarrhea	**la diarrea** lah dee·ahr·_reh_·ah	
an earache	**mal d'orecchio** mahl doh·_rehk_·kyoh	
a fever	**la febbre** lah _fehb_·breh	
pain	**un dolore** oon doh·_loh_·reh	
a rash	**un rossore** oon rohs·_soh_·reh	
a sting	**una puntura** _oo_·nah poon·_too_·rah	
a sprain	**una storta** _oo_·nah _stohr_·tah	
some swelling	**un gonfiore** oon gohn·_fyoh_·reh	
a sore throat	**il mal di gola** eel mahl dee _goh_·lah	
a stomach ache	**mal di stomaco** mahl dee _stoh_·mah·koh	
sunstroke	**l'insolazione** leen·soh·lah·_tsyoh_·neh	
I've been sick [ill] for...days.	**Sto male da...giorni.** stoh _mah_·leh dah... _jyohr_·nee	

Conditions

I'm...	**Sono...** _soh_•noh...
anemic	**anemico** m **/anemica** f ah•_neh_•mee•koh/ ah•_neh_•mee•kah
asthmatic	**asmatico** m **/asmatica** f ahz•_mah_•tee•koh/ ahz•_mah_•tee•kah
diabetic	**diabetico** m **/diabetica** f dee•ah•_beh_•tee•koh/ dee•ah•_beh_•tee•kah
epileptic	**epilettico** m **/epilettica** f eh•pee•leht•tee•koh/ eh•pee•leht•tee•kah
I'm allergic to antibiotics/ penicillin.	**Sono allergico** m **/allergica** f **agli antibiotici/alla penicillina.** _soh_•noh ahl•_lehr_•jee•koh/ahl•_lehr_•jee•kah ah•llyee ahn•tee•_byoh_•tee•chee/_ahl_•lah peh•nee•cheel•_lee_•nah
I have...	**Soffro di...** _sohf_•froh dee...
arthritis	**artrite** ahr•_tree_•teh
a heart condition	**cuore** _kwoh_•reh
high/low blood pressure	**alta/bassa pressione** _ahl_•tah/_bahs_•sah prehs•_syoh_•neh
I'm on...	**Prendo...** _prehn_•doh...

Treatment

Do I need a prescription/medicine?	**Ci vuole la ricetta?** chee vwoh•leh lah ree•cheht•tah?
Can you prescribe a generic drug [unbranded medication]?	**Mi può prescrivere un medicinale generico?** mee pwoh preh•skree•veh•reh oon meh•dee•chee•nah•leh jeh•neh•ree•koh
Where can I get it?	**Dove lo posso trovare?** doh•veh loh pohs•soh troh•vah•reh?

Hospital

Notify my family, please.	**Avvisi la mia famiglia, per favore.** *ahv‑vee‑zee lah mee‑ah fah‑mee‑llyah pehr fah‑voh‑reh*
I'm in pain.	**Sto male.** *stoh mah‑leh*
I need a doctor/nurse.	**Ho bisogno di un medico/un'infermiera.** *oh bee‑zoh‑nyoh dee oon meh‑dee‑koh/ oo‑neen‑fehr‑myeh‑rah*
When are visiting hours?	**Qual è l'orario delle visite?** *kwahl eh loh‑rah‑ryoh dehl‑leh vee‑zee‑teh*
I'm visiting…	**Sto visitando…** *stoh vee‑zee‑tahn‑doh…*

YOU MAY HEAR…

Cosa c'è che non va? *koh‑zah cheh keh nohn vah*	What's wrong?
Dove le fa male? *doh‑veh leh fah mah‑leh*	Where does it hurt?
Fa male qui? *fah mah‑leh kwee*	Does it hurt here?
Prende farmaci? *prehn‑deh fahr‑mah‑chee*	Are you on medication?
Ha allergie? *ah ahl‑lehr‑jee‑eh*	Are you allergic to anything?
Apra la bocca. *ah‑prah lah bohk‑kah*	Open your mouth.
Respiri profondamente. *reh‑spee‑ree proh‑fohn‑dah‑mehn‑teh*	Breathe deeply.
Vada in ospedale. *vah‑dah een oh‑speh‑dah‑leh*	Go to the hospital.
È… *eh…*	It's…
rotto *roht‑toh*	broken
contagioso *kohn‑tah‑jyoh‑zoh*	contagious
infetto *een‑feht‑toh*	infected
È una storta. *eh oo‑nah stohr‑tah*	It's sprained.
Niente di grave. *nyehn‑teh dee grah‑veh*	It's nothing serious.

Dentist

I have a broken tooth.	**Ho un dente rotto.** *oh oon dehn·teh roht·toh*
I have lost a filling.	**Ho perso un'otturazione.** *oh pehr·soh oo·noht·too·rah·tsyoh·neh*
I have a toothache.	**Ho mal di denti.** *oh mahl dee dehn·tee*
Can you fix this denture?	**Può aggiustare la dentiera?** *pwoh ah·djoo·stah·reh lah dehn·tyeh·rah*

Gynecologist

I have cramps/ a vaginal infection.	**Ho i crampi/un'infezione vaginale.** *oh ee krahm·pee/oo·neen·feh·tsyoh·neh vah·jee·nah·leh*
I missed my period.	**Non ho avuto il ciclo.** *nohn oh ah·voo·toh eel chee·kloh*
I'm on the Pill.	**Prendo la pillola.** *prehn·doh lah peel·loh·lah*
I'm (not) pregnant.	**(Non) Sono incinta.** *(nohn) soh·noh een·cheen·tah*
My last period was…	**Ho avuto l'ultimo ciclo…** *oh ah·voo·toh lool·tee·moh chee·kloh…*

Optician

I've lost…	**Ho perso…** *oh pehr·soh…*
a contact lens	**una lente a contatto** *oo·nah lehn·teh ah kohn·taht·toh*
my glasses	**gli occhiali** *lyee ohk·kyah·lee*
a lens	**una lente** *oo·nah lehn·teh*

Payment & Insurance

How much?	**Quanto costa?** *kwahn·toh koh·stah*
Can I pay by credit card?	**Posso pagare con carta di credito?** *poh·soh pah·gah·reh kohn kahr·tah dee kreh·dee·toh*
I have insurance.	**Ho l'assicurazione.** *oh lahs·see·koo·rah·tsyoh·neh*
I need a receipt. for my insurance.	**Mi serve una ricevuta per l'assicurazione.** *mee sehr·veh oo·nah ree·cheh·voo·tah pehr lahs·see·koo·rah·tsyoh·neh*

Pharmacy

ESSENTIAL

Where's the pharmacy?	**Dov'è una farmacia?** *doh•veh oo•nah fahr•mah•chee•ah*
What time does it open/close?	**A che ora apre/chiude?** *ah keh oh•rah ah•preh/kyoo•deh*
What would you recommend for…?	**Cosa consiglierebbe per…?** *koh•zah kohn•see•llyeh•rehb•beh pehr…*
How much do I take?	**Quanto ne prendo?** *kwahn•toh neh prehn•doh*
Can you fill [make up] this prescription?	**Può darmi questo farmaco?** *pwoh dahr•mee kweh•stoh fahr•mah•koh*
I'm allergic to…	**Sono allergico** *m* /**allergica** *f* **a…** *soh•noh ahl•lehr•jee•koh/ahl•lehr•jee•kah ah…*

What to Take

How much do I take?	**Quanto ne prendo?**	_kwahn_•toh neh _prehn_•doh
How often?	**Con che frequenza?**	_kohn keh freh•_kwehn_•tsah_
Is it safe for children?	**È per bambini?**	_eh pehr bahm•_bee_•nee_
I'm taking…	**Prendo…**	_prehn_•doh…
Are there side effects?	**Ha effetti collaterali?**	_ah ehf•_feht_•tee kohl•_lah_•teh•_rah_•lee_
I need something for…	**Ho bisogno di qualcosa per…**	_oh bee•_soh_•nyoh dee kwahl•_koh_•zah pehr…_
a cold	**il raffreddore**	_eel_ rahf_•frehd•_doh_•reh_
a cough	**la tosse**	_lah_ tohs_•seh_
diarrhea	**la diarrea**	_lah dee•ahr•_reh_•ah_
a headache	**il mal di testa**	_eel mahl dee tehs•tah_
insect bites	**una puntura d'insetto**	_oo_•nah poon•_too_•rah deen•_seht_•toh_
car/sea/air motion [travel] sickness	**il mal d'auto/di mare/d'aria**	_eel mahl_ dow•toh/dee _mah_•reh/_dah_•ryah_
a sore throat	**il mal di gola**	_eel mahl dee_ goh_•lah_
sunburn	**una scottatura**	_oo_•nah _skoht_•tah•_too_•rah_
toothache	**Il mal di denti**	_eel mahl dee dehn•tee_
an upset stomach	**lo stomaco in disordine**	_loh_ stoh_•mah•koh een dee•_zohr_•dee•neh_

Pharmacies are usually open from 8:30 a.m. 12:30 p.m. and 3:30 p.m. 7:30 p.m. In larger cities there is often a **farmacia di turno** available; this pharmacy will have extended hours during the week, weekend and on holidays.
In an emergency, dial 118 for an ambulance.

YOU MAY SEE...

UNA/TRE VOLTE AL GIORNO	once/three times a day
COMPRESSA	tablet
GOCCIA	drop
CUCCHIAINO	teaspoon
DOPO I/PRIMA DEI/CON I PASTI	after/before/with meals
A STOMACO VUOTO	on an empty stomach
DA INGHIOTTIRE INTERA	swallow whole
PUÒ PROVOCARE SONNOLENZA	may cause drowsiness
SOLO PER USO ESTERNO	for external use only

Basic Supplies

I'd like...	**Vorrei...** vohr·_ray_...
acetaminophen [paracetamol]	**del paracetamolo** dehl pah·rah·cheh·tah·_moh_·loh
antiseptic cream	**una crema antisettica** _oo_·nah _kreh_·mah _ahn_·tee·_seht_·tee·kah
aspirin	**dell'aspirina** dehl·_lah_·spee·_ree_·nah
bandages	**delle fasce** _dehl_·leh _fah_·sheh
a comb	**un pettine** oon _peht_·tee·neh
condoms	**dei preservativi** day preh·sehr·vah·_tee_·vee
contact lens solution	**una soluzione per le lenti a contatto** _oo_·nah soh·loo·_tsyoh_·neh pehr leh _lehn_·tee ah kohn·_taht_·toh
deodorant	**un deodorante** oon deh·oh·doh·_rahn_·teh
a hairbrush	**una spazzola** _oo_·nah _spah_·tsoh·lah
hairspray	**una lacca** _oo_·nah _lahk_·kah
ibuprofen	**dell'ibuprofene** dehl·lee·boo·proh·_feh_·neh

insect repellent	**un repellente per gli insetti** *oon reh•pehl•<u>lehn</u>•teh pehr llyeen•<u>seht</u>•tee*	
lotion	**una lozione** *<u>oo</u>•nah loh•<u>tsyoh</u>•neh*	
a nail file	**una limetta per le unghie** *<u>oo</u>•nah <u>lee</u>•meht•tah pehr leh <u>oon</u>•ghyeh*	
soap	**una saponetta** *<u>oo</u>•nah sah•poh•<u>neht</u>•tah*	
a (disposable) razor	**una lametta (usa e getta)** *<u>oo</u>•nah lah•<u>meht</u>•tah (<u>oo</u>•zah eh <u>jeht</u>•tah)*	
razor blades	**delle lamette per rasoio** *<u>dehl</u>•leh lah•<u>meht</u>•teh pehr rah•<u>zoh</u>•yoh*	161
sanitary napkins [towels]	**un pacco di assorbenti** *oon pahk•<u>koh</u> dee ahs•sohr•<u>behn</u>•tee*	
shampoo/ conditioner	**uno shampoo/un balsamo** *<u>oo</u>•noh shahm•<u>pooh</u>/oon bahl•sah•moh*	
sunscreen	**un filtro solare** *oon <u>feel</u>•troh soh•<u>lah</u>•reh*	
tampons	**una scatola di tamponi** *<u>oo</u>•nah <u>ska</u>•toh•lah dee tahm•<u>poh</u>•nee*	
tissues	**dei fazzoletti di carta** *day fah•tsoh•<u>leht</u>•tee dee <u>kahr</u>•tah*	
toilet paper	**della carta igienica** *<u>dehl</u>•lah <u>kahr</u>•tah ee•<u>jyeh</u>•nee•kah*	
toothpaste	**un dentifricio** *oon dehn•tee•<u>free</u>•chyoh*	

For Baby Essentials, see page 145.

The Basics

Grammar

In Italian, there are four forms for 'you' (taking different verb forms): **tu** (singular) and **voi** (plural) are used informally, when talking to relatives, close friends and children (and among young people); the polite form **Lei** (singular) and **loro** (plural) are used in all other cases. If in doubt, use **Lei/loro**. The following abbreviations are used in this section: sing. = singular; pl. = plural; inf. = informal; for. = formal.

Regular Verbs

There are three verb types: infinitives ending in **-are**, **-ere** and **-ire**, e.g. **parlare** (to speak), **vendere** (to sell) and **dormire** (to sleep). Following are sample conjugations for each verb type.

PARLARE (to speak, to talk)		Present	Past	Future
I	**io**	parl**o**	ho parlato	parl**erò**
you (sing.) (inf.)	**tu**	parl**i**	hai parlato	parl**erai**
he/she/you (sing.) (for.)	**lui/lei/Lei**	parl**a**	ha parlato	parl**erà**
we	**noi**	parl**iamo**	abbiamo parlato	parl**eremo**
you (pl.) (inf.)	**voi**	parl**ate**	avete parlato	parl**erete**
they/you (pl.) (for.)	**loro**	parl**ano**	hanno parlato	parl**eranno**

VENDERE (to sell)		Present	Past	Future
I	**io**	vend**o**	ho venduto	vend**erò**
you (sing.) (inf.)	**tu**	vend**i**	hai venduto	vend**erai**
he/she/you (sing.) (for.)	**lui/lei/Lei**	vend**e**	ha venduto	vend**erà**

we	**noi**	vend**iamo**	abbiamo venduto	vend**eremo**
you (pl.) (inf.)	**voi**	vend**ete**	avete venduto	vend**erete**
they/you (pl.) (for.)	**loro**	vend**ono**	hanno venduto	vend**eranno**

DORMIRE (to sleep)		**Present**	**Past**	**Future**
I	**io**	dorm**o**	ho dormito	dorm**irò**
you (sing.) (inf.)	**tu**	dorm**i**	hai dormito	dorm**irai**
he/she/you (sing.) (for.)	**lui/lei/Lei**	dorm**e**	ha dormito	dorm**irà**
we	**noi**	dorm**iamo**	abbiamo dormito	dorm**iremo**
you (pl.) (inf.)	**voi**	dorm**ite**	avete dormito	dorm**irete**
they/you (pl.) (for.)	**loro**	dorm**ono**	hanno dormito	dorm**iranno**

Irregular Verbs

There are many irregular verbs whose forms do not follow the regular patterns. The following are the present, past and future forms of **essere** (to be) and **avere** (to have).

ESSERE (to be)		**Present**	**Past**	**Future**
I	**io**	sono	sono stato	sarò
you (sing.) (inf.)	**tu**	sei	sei stato	sarai
he/she/you (sing.) (for)	**lui/lei/Lei**	è	è stato	sarà
we	**noi**	siamo	siamo stati	saremo
you (pl.) (inf.)	**voi**	siete	siete stati	sarete
they/you (pl.) (for.)	**loro**	sono	sono stati	saranno

AVERE (to have)			Present	Past	Future
I	**io**	ho	ho avuto	avrò
you (sing.) (inf.)	**tu**	hai	hai avuto	avrai
he/she/you (sing.) (for)	**lui/lei/Lei**	ha	ha avuto	avrà
we	**noi**	abbiamo	abbiamo avuto	avremo
you (pl.) (inf.)	**voi**	avete	avete avuto	avrete
they/you (pl.) (for.) **loro**		hanno	hanno avuto	avranno

Word Order

Italian sentences generally follow the subject-verb-object pattern, as in English.

Example: **Vorrei un taxi subito.** I'd like a taxi now.

In Italian, adjectives usually follow the noun.

Example: **un'auto economica** a cheap car (literally, a car cheap)

To form a question in Italian, you can raise the intonation at the end of the sentence, as in English, or use a question word.

Examples:

Lei parla italiano./Lei parla italiano?

You speak Italian./Do you speak Italian?

Quanto costa?

How much?

Negations

To form the negative, use **non** before the conjugated verb.

Example: **Parlo inglese./Non parlo inglese.**

I speak English./I don't speak English.

Imperatives

The imperative, or command form, of Italian verbs is used to give orders or advice. Signs are often in the imperative form. It is formed by adding a specific ending to the stem of the verb (add **–i** to **–are** verbs, and **–a** to **–ere** and **–**

ire verbs). To say the negative, add **non** before the verb. The following are the polite ways to say common commands in Italian:

Fermi!	**Avanti!**	**Non parli!**
Stop!	Go!	Don't speak!

To say 'Let's...' add **–iamo** to the stem of the verb.

Andiamo!	**Finiamo!**
Let's go!	Let's finish!

Nouns & Articles

Generally nouns ending in **–o** are masculine, their plural ending changing to **–i**. Those ending in **–a** are usually feminine, their plural ending changing to **–e**. Nouns ending in **–e** can be either gender changing to **–i** in the plural. The definite articles (the) are **il** m and **la** f; **l'** is used for singular masculine or feminine nouns that begin with a vowel. The plural forms are **I** m and **le** f. When a masculine noun begins with **z** or **s** + consonant, the singular article changes to **lo**, the plural to **gli**. **Gli** is also used before plural masculine nouns that begin with a vowel.

The indefinite articles (a, an) also indicate gender: a masculine noun uses **un**, or **uno** when the noun begins with **z** or **s** + consonant. The feminine noun takes **una**, or **un'** when the noun begins with a vowel.

When prepositions are followed by definite articles, they sometimes combine to form one word. For example: **di + el = del**; **di + lo = dello**; **di + l' = dell'**; **di + i = dei**; **di + gli = degli**; **di + la = della**; **di + le = delle**.

Adjectives

Adjectives modify nouns and must agree with the noun in both gender and number. Adjectives ending in **–o** can have four forms, matching the noun:

Masculine, singular: end in **–o: ragazzo italiano** (Italian boy)
Masculine, plural: end in **–i: ragazzi italiani** (Italian boys)
Feminine, singular: end in **–a: signora italiana** (Italian woman)
Feminine, plural: end in **–e: signore italiane** (Italian women)

Adjectives ending in **–e** are the same for masculine and feminine singular, and change to **–i** in the masculine and feminine plural forms.

Example: **ragazzo inglese** (English boy); **ragazza inglese** (English girl); **ragazzi inglesi** (English boys); **ragazze inglesi** (English girls)

Comparatives & Superlatives

To say 'more', use **più**. To say 'less' use **meno**. To say 'the most' or 'the least', use **più** or **meno**, respectively, preceded by the definite article.

Examples:

casa grande/casa più grande/la casa più grande

large house/larger house/the largest house

borsa piccola/borsa più piccola/la borsa più piccola

small bag/smaller bag/the smallest bag

Possessive Pronouns & Adjectives

The following are the Italian forms of possessive pronouns/adjectives. Note that the gender and number agree with the noun, not the speaker.

	masculine, singular	masculine, plural	feminine, singular	feminine, plural
my, mine	**il mio**	**i miei**	**la mia**	**le mie**
your, yours	**il tuo**	**i tuoi**	**la tua**	**le tue**
his, her, hers, its, yours (sing.) (for.)	**il suo**	**i suoi**	**la sua**	**le sue**
our, ours	**il nostro**	**i nostri**	**la nostra**	**le nostre**
your, yours	**il vostro**	**i vostri**	**la vostra**	**le vostre**
their, theirs, yours (pl.) (for.)	**il loro**	**i loro**	**la loro**	**le loro**

Adverbs & Adverbial Expressions

Some Italian adverbs are formed by adding **–mente** to the feminine singular form of the adjective.

Example: **lento** *m* /**lenta** *f* (slow), **lentamente** (slowly)

If the adjective ends in **–le** or **–re**, drop the **–e** and add **–mente**.

Example: **facile** (easy), **facilmente** (easily)

Numbers

ESSENTIAL

0	**zero**	*dzeh•roh*
1	**uno**	*oo•noh*
2	**due**	*doo•eh*
3	**tre**	*treh*
4	**quattro**	*kwaht•troh*
5	**cinque**	*cheen•kweh*
6	**sei**	*say*
7	**sette**	*seht•teh*
8	**otto**	*oht•toh*
9	**nove**	*noh•veh*
10	**dieci**	*dyeh•chee*
11	**undici**	*oon•dee•chee*
12	**dodici**	*doh•dee•chee*
13	**tredici**	*treh•dee•chee*
14	**quattordici**	*kwaht•tohr•dee•chee*
15	**quindici**	*kween•dee•chee*
16	**sedici**	*seh•dee•chee*
17	**diciassette**	*dee•chyahs•seht•teh*
18	**diciotto**	*dee•chyoht•toh*
19	**diciannove**	*dee•chyahn•noh•veh*

20	**venti** _vehn_·tee
21	**ventuno** vehn·_too_·noh
22	**ventidue** vehn·tee·_doo_·eh
30	**trenta** _trehn_·tah
31	**trentuno** trehn·_too_·noh
40	**quaranta** kwah·_rahn_·tah
50	**cinquanta** cheen·_kwahn_·tah
60	**sessanta** sehs·_sahn_·tah
70	**settanta** seht·_tahn_·tah
80	**ottanta** oht·_tahn_·tah
90	**novanta** noh·_vahn_·tah
100	**cento** _chehn_·toh
101	**centuno** chehn·_too_·noh
200	**duecento** doo·eh·_chehn_·toh
500	**cinquecento** cheen·kweh·_chehn_·toh
1,000	**mille** _meel_·leh
10,000	**diecimila** dyeh·chee·_mee_·lah
1,000,000	**milione** mee·_lyoh_·neh

Ordinal Numbers

first	**primo** _pree_·moh
second	**secondo** seh·_kohn_·doh
third	**terzo** _tehr_·tsoh
fourth	**quarto** _kwahr_·toh
fifth	**quinto** _kween_·toh
once	**una volta** _oo_·nah _vohl_·tah
twice	**due volte** _doo_·eh _vohl_·teh
three times	**tre volte** treh _vohl_·teh

Time

ESSENTIAL

What time is it?	**Che ore sono?** keh <u>oh</u>•reh <u>soh</u>•noh	
It's noon [midday].	**È mezzogiorno.** eh meh•dzoh•<u>jyohr</u>•noh	
At midnight.	**A mezzanotte.** ah meh•dzah•<u>noht</u>•teh	
From one o'clock to two o'clock.	**Dall'una alle due.** dahl•<u>loo</u>•nah <u>ahl</u>•leh <u>doo</u>•eh	
Five after [past] three.	**Le tre e cinque.** leh treh eh <u>cheen</u>•kweh	
A quarter to three.	**Sono le tre meno un quarto.** <u>soh</u>•noh leh treh <u>meh</u>•noh oon <u>kwahr</u>•toh	
5:30 a.m./5:30 p.m.	**le cinque e mezzo/le diciassette e trenta** leh <u>cheen</u>•kweh eh <u>meh</u>•dzoh/ leh <u>dee</u>•chyahs•<u>seht</u>•teh eh <u>trehn</u>•tah	

Days

ESSENTIAL

Monday	**lunedì** loon•eh•<u>dee</u>	
Tuesday	**martedì** mahr•teh•<u>dee</u>	
Wednesday	**mercoledì** mehr•koh•leh•<u>dee</u>	
Thursday	**giovedì** jyoh•veh•<u>dee</u>	
Friday	**venerdì** veh•nehr•<u>dee</u>	
Saturday	**sabato** <u>sah</u>•bah•toh	
Sunday	**domenica** doh•<u>meh</u>•nee•kah	

Dates

yesterday	**ieri** _yeh_·ree
today	**oggi** _oh_·djee
tomorrow	**domani** doh·_mah_·nee
day	**giorno** _jyohr_·noh
week	**settimana** seht·tee·_mah_·nah
month	**mese** _meh_·zeh
year	**anno** _ahn_·noh

Months

January	**gennaio** jehn·_nah_·yoh
February	**febbraio** fehb·_brah_·yoh
March	**marzo** _mahr_·tsoh
April	**aprile** ah·_pree_·leh
May	**maggio** _mah_·djoh
June	**giugno** _jyoo_·nyoh
July	**luglio** _loo_·llyoh
August	**agosto** ah·_goh_·stoh
September	**settembre** seht·_tehm_·breh
October	**ottobre** oht·_toh_·breh
November	**novembre** noh·_vehm_·breh
December	**dicembre** dee·_chem_·breh

Lunedì (Monday) is the first day of the week; **domenica** (Sunday) is the last. Italian does not capitalize the names of days.

Italy follows a day-month-year format instead of the month-day-year format used in the U.S.
For example, July 25, 2008; 25/07/08 = 7/25/2008 in the U.S.

Seasons

in/during...	**in/durante...**	*een/doo·rahn·teh...*
the spring	**la primavera**	*lah pree·mah·veh·rah*
the summer	**l'estate**	*leh·stah·teh*
the fall [autumn]	**l'autunno**	*l·ow·toon·noh*
the winter	**l'inverno**	*leen·vehr·noh*

Holidays

January 1: **Capodanno** New Year's Day

January 6: **Epifania** Epiphany

April 25: **Festa della Liberazione** Liberation Day

May 1: **Festa dei Lavoratori** Labor Day

August 15: **Ferragosto** Assumption Day

November 1: **Ognissanti** All Saints Day

December 8: **Immacolata Concezione** Immaculate Conception

December 25: **Natale** Christmas Day

December 26: **Santo Stefano** St. Stephen's Day

Moveable dates include:

Venerdì Santo Good Friday

Pasqua Easter Day

Pasquetta Easter Monday

Conversion Tables

When you know	Multiply by	To find
ounces	*28.3*	grams
pounds	*0.45*	kilograms
inches	*2.54*	centimeters
feet	*0.3*	meters
miles	*1.61*	kilometers
square inches	*6.45*	sq. centimeters
square feet	*0.09*	sq. meters
square miles	*2.59*	sq. kilometers
pints (U.S./Brit)	*0.47/0.56*	liters
gallons (U.S./Brit)	*3.8/4.5*	liters
Fahrenheit	*5/9, after 32*	Centigrade
Centigrade	*9/5, then +32*	Fahrenheit

Kilometers to Miles Conversions

1 km – 0.62 mi	**20 km** – 12.4 mi
5 km – 3.10 mi	**50 km** – 31.0 mi
10 km – 6.20 mi	**100 km** – 61.0 mi

Measurement

1 gram (gr)	**1 grammo**	= 0.035 oz.
1/10 of a kilo	**etto** (sing.)/**etti** (pl.)	= 0.22 lb
1 kilogram (kg)	**1 chilo**	= 2.2 lb
1 liter (l)	**1 litro**	= 1.06 U.S./ 0.88 Brit. quarts
1 centimeter (cm)	**1 centimetro**	= 0.4 inch
1 meter (m)	**1 metro**	= 3.28 ft.
1 kilometer (km)	**1 chilometro**	= 0.62 mile

Temperature

-40° C – -40° F	**-1**° C – 30° F	**20**° C – 68° F
-30° C – -22° F	**0**° C – 32° F	**25**° C – 77° F
-20° C – -4° F	**5**° C – 41° F	**30**° C – 86° F
-10° C – 14° F	**10**° C – 50° F	**35**° C – 95° F
-5° C – 23° F	**15**° C – 59° F	

Oven Temperature

100° C – 212° F	**177**° C – 350° F
121° C – 250° F	**204**° C – 400° F
149° C – 300° F	**260**° C – 500° F

Dictionary

English–Italian 175
Italian–English 200

English–Italian

A

a.m. del mattino
abbey l'abbazia
accept v accettare
access l'accesso
accident l'incidente
accommodation l'alloggio
account il conto
acupuncture l'agopuntura
adapter l'adattatore
address l'indirizzo
admission l'ingresso
after dopo; **~noon** il pomeriggio; **~shave** il dopobarba
age l'età
agency l'agenzia
AIDS l'AIDS
air l'aria; **~ conditioning** l'aria condizionata; **~ pump** la pompa dell'aria; **~line** la compagnia aerea; **~mail** la posta aerea; **~plane** l'aereo; **~port** l'aeroporto
aisle il corridoio; **~ seat** il posto sul corridoio

allergic allergico; **~ reaction** la reazione allergica
allow v permettere
alone solo
alter v modificare
alternate route il percorso alternativo
aluminum foil la carta stagnola
amazing straordinario
ambulance l'ambulanza
American americano
amusement park il lunapark
and and
anemic anemico
anesthesia l'anestesia
animal l'animale
ankle la caviglia
antibiotic l'antibiotico
antiques store il negozio d'antiquariato
antiseptic cream la crema antisettica
anything qualsiasi cosa
apartment l'appartamento
appendix (body part) l'appendice

adj adjective	**BE** British English	**v** verb
adv adverb	**n** noun	

appetizer l'antipasto
appointment l'appuntamento
arcade la sala giochi
area code il prefisso
arm il braccio
aromatherapy l'aromaterapia
around (the corner) dietro di
arrivals (airport) gli arrivi
arrive v arrivare
artery l'arteria
arthritis l'artrite
art l'arte
aspirin l'aspirina
asthmatic asmatico
ATM il bancomat
attack l'aggressione
attend v frequentare
attraction (place) l'attrattiva
attractive attraente
Australia Australia
Australian australiano
automatic automatico; ~ **car**
l'auto col cambio automatico
available libero

B

baby il bebè; ~ **bottle** il biberon;
~ **wipe** la salvietta per neonati;
~**sitter** la babysitter
back (body part) la schiena;
~**ache** il mal di schiena;

~**pack** lo zaino
bag la borsa
baggage il bagaglio; ~ **claim** il
ritiro bagagli; ~ **ticket** lo
scontrino bagagli
bakery la panetteria
ballet lo spettacolo di danza
bandage la benda
bank la banca
bar il bar
barbecue il barbecue
barber il barbiere
baseball il baseball
basket (grocery store) il cestino
basketball il basketball
bathroom il bagno
battery la batteria
battleground il campo di battaglia
be v essere
beach la spiaggia
beautiful bello
bed il letto; ~ **and breakfast**
la pensione
begin v iniziare
before prima
beginner il principiante
behind dietro
beige beige
belt la cintura
berth la cuccetta
best il migliore

better migliore
bicycle la bicicletta
big grande
bigger più grande
bike route il percorso ciclabile
bikini il bikini; **~ wax** la ceretta all'inguine
bill v (charge) fatturare;
  ~ n (money) la banconota;
  ~ n (of sale) il conto
bird l'uccello
birthday il compleanno
black nero
bladder la vescica
bland insipido
blanket la coperta
bleed v sanguinare
blood il sangue; **~ pressure** la pressione sanguigna
blouse la camicetta
blue blu
board v imbarcarsi
boarding pass la carta d'imbarco
boat la barca
bone l'osso
book il libro; **~store** la libreria
boots gli stivali
boring noioso
botanical garden il giardino botanico
bother v infastidire

bottle la bottiglia;
  ~ opener l'apribottiglie
bowl la coppa
box la scatola
boxing match l'incontro di boxe
boy il ragazzo; **~friend** il ragazzo
bra il reggiseno
bracelet il braccialetto
brakes (car) i freni
break v rompere; **~-in (burglary)** il furto con scasso;
  ~down il guasto
breakfast la colazione
breast il petto; **~feed** v allattare
breathe v respirare
bridge il ponte
briefs (clothing) lo slip
bring v portare
British britannico(a)
broken rotto
brooch la spilla
broom la scopa
brother il fratello
brown marrone
bug l'insetto
building l'edificio
burn v bruciare
bus l'autobus; **~ station** la stazione degli autobus;
  ~ stop la fermata del bus;
  ~ ticket il biglietto del bus;

~ **tour** l'escursione in pullman
business il lavoro; ~ **card** il biglietto da visita; ~ **center** il centro business; ~ **class** la classe business; ~ **hours** l'orario d'apertura
butcher il macellaio
buttocks le natiche
buy v comprare
bye ciao

C

cabaret il cabaret
cabin la cabina
cable car la funivia
cafe il caffè
call v chiamare; ~ n la chiamata
calories le calorie
camera la macchina fotografica; **digital** ~ la macchina fotografica digitale; ~ **case** l'astuccio della macchina fotografica; ~ **store** il negozio di fotografia
camp v campeggiare; ~ **stove** il fornello da campeggio; ~**site** il campeggio
can opener l'apriscatole
Canada il Canada
Canadian canadese
cancel v annullare
candy le caramelle

canned good lo scatolame
canyon il canalone
car l'auto; ~ **hire** [BE] l'autonoleggio; ~ **park** [BE] il parcheggio; ~ **rental** l'autonoleggio; ~ **seat** il seggiolino per auto
carafe la caraffa
card la carta; **ATM** ~ il bancomat; **credit** ~ la carta di credito; **debit** ~ il bancomat; **phone** ~ la scheda telefonica
carry on board v [BE] portare a bordo
carry-on il bagaglio a mano
cart (grocery store) il carrello; ~ **(luggage)** il carrello
carton il cartone; ~ **of cigarettes** la stecca di sigarette
case (container) la cassa
cash v incassare; ~ n i contanti; ~ **advance** l'acconto
cashier il cassiere
casino il casinò
castle il castello
cathedral la cattedrale
cave la grotta
CD il CD
cell phone il telefonino
Celsius Celsius
centimeter il centimetro

certificate il certificato
chair la sedia; **~ lift** la seggiovia
change v (**buses**) cambiare;
 ~ v (**money**) cambiare;
 ~ v (**baby**) cambiare;
 ~ n (**money**) il cambio
charcoal il carbone
charge v (**credit card**) addebitare;
 ~ n (**cost**) il costo
cheap economico; **~er** più
 economico
check v (**on something**)
 controllare; **~** v (**luggage**)
 controllare; **~** n (**payment**)
 l'assegno; **~-in** (**hotel/airport**)
 il check-in; **~ing account**
 il conto corrente; **~-out** (**hotel**)
 il pagamento del conto
Cheers! Salute!
chemical toilet il WC da
 campeggio
chemist [BE] la farmacia
cheque [BE] l'assegno
chest (**body part**) il petto;
 ~ pain il dolore al petto
chewing gum la gomma da
 masticare
child il bambino; **~ seat** il
 seggiolone; **~'s menu** il menù per
 bambino; **~'s portion** la porzione
 per bambino

Chinese cinese
chopsticks i bastoncini cinesi
church la chiesa
cigar il sigaro
cigarette la sigaretta
class la classe; **business ~**
 la classe business; **economy ~**
 la classe economica; **first ~**
 la prima classe
classical music la musica classica
clean v pulire; **~** adj pulito; **~ing**
 product il prodotto per la pulizia;
 ~ing supplies i prodotti per la
 pulizia
clear v (**on an ATM**) cancellare
cliff la scogliera
cling film [BE] la pellicola per
 alimenti
close v (**a shop**) chiudere
close vicino
closed chiuso
clothing l'abbigliamento;
 ~ store il negozio
 d'abbigliamento
club il club
coat il cappotto
coffee shop il caffè
coin la moneta
colander la scolapasta
cold (**sickness**) il raffreddore;
 ~ (**temperature**) freddo

colleague il collega
cologne la colonia
color il colore
comb il pettine
come v venire
complaint il reclamo
computer il computer
concert il concerto; ~ **hall** la sala da concerti
condition (medical) la condizione
conditioner il balsamo
condom il preservativo
conference la conferenza
confirm v confermare
congestion la congestione
connect v (internet) collegarsi
connection (internet) il collegamento; ~ **(flight)** la coincidenza
constipated costipato
consulate il consolato
consultant il consulente
contact v contattare; ~ **lens** la lente a contatto; ~ **lens solution** la soluzione per lenti a contatto
contagious contagioso
convention hall la sala congressi
conveyor belt il nastro trasportatore
cook v cucinare

cooking gas il gas per cucina
cool (temperature) fresco
copper il rame
corkscrew il cavatappi
cost v costare
cot il lettino
cotton il cotone
cough v tossire; ~ n la tosse
country code il prefisso del paese
cover charge il coperto
crash v (car) fare un incidente
cream (ointment) la crema
credit card la carta di credito
crew neck a girocollo
crib la culla
crystal il cristallo
cup la tazza
currency la valuta; ~ **exchange** il cambio valuta; ~ **exchange office** l'ufficio di cambio
current account [BE] il conto corrente
customs la dogana
cut v (hair) tagliare; ~ n (injury) il taglio
cute carino
cycling il ciclismo

D

damage v danneggiare; ~**d** danneggiato

dance v ballare; **~ club** il club di ballo; **~ing** il ballo
dangerous pericoloso
dark scuro
date (calendar) la data
day il giorno
deaf sordo
debit card il bancomat
deck chair la sedia a sdraio
declare v dichiarare
decline v **(credit card)** rifiutare
deeply profondamente
degrees (temperature) i gradi
delay v ritardare
delete v **(computer)** eliminare
delicatessen la gastronomia
delicious squisito
denim i jeans
dentist il dentista
denture la dentiera
deodorant il deodorante
department store il grande magazzino
departures (airport) le partenze
deposit v depositare;
 ~ (bank) n il deposito;
 ~ (to reserve a room) il deposito
desert il deserto
detergent il detersivo
develop v **(film)** sviluppare
diabetic diabetico

dial v comporre il numero
diamond il diamante
diaper il pannolino
diarrhea la diarrea
diesel il diesel
difficult difficile
digital digitale; **~ camera** la macchina fotografica digitale;
 ~ photos le foto digitali;
 ~ prints le stampe digitali
dining room la sala da pranzo
dinner la cena
direction la direzione
dirty sporco
disabled il disabile; **~ accessible [BE]** accessibile ai disabili
disconnect v **(computer)** scollegare
discount lo sconto
dish (kitchen) il piatto;
 ~washer la lavastoviglie;
 ~washing liquid il detersivo per i piatti
display lo schermo; **~ case** la vetrinetta
disposable usa e getta; **~ razor** la lametta usa e getta
dive v tuffarsi; **~ing equipment** l'attrezzatura subacquea
divorce v divorziare
dizzy stordito

doctor il medico
doll la bambola
dollar (U.S.) il dollaro
domestic domestico; ~ **flight** il volo nazionale
door la porta
dormitory il dormitorio
double bed il letto matrimoniale
downtown (direction) il centro; ~ **area** il centro
dozen la dozzina
drag lift lo ski lift
dress (piece of clothing) il vestito; ~ **code** il codice di abbigliamento
drink v bere; ~ n la bevanda; ~ **menu** il menù delle bevande; ~**ing water** l'acqua potabile
drive v guidare
driver's license number il numero di patente
drop (medicine) la goccia
drowsiness la sonnolenza
dry cleaner il lavasecco
dubbed doppiato
during durante
duty (tax) la tassa; ~ **free** duty free
DVD il DVD

E

ear l'orecchio; ~**ache** il mal d'orecchio
earlier prima
early presto
earrings gli orecchini
east est
easy facile
eat v mangiare
economy class la classe economica
elbow il gomito
electric outlet la presa elettrica
elevator l'ascensore
e-mail v inviare e-mail; ~ n l'e-mail; ~ **address** l'indirizzo e-mail
emergency l'emergenza; ~ **exit** l'uscita d'emergenza
empty v svuotare
enamel (jewelry) lo smalto
end v finire
English inglese
engrave v incidere
enjoy v godersi
enter v entrare
entertainment l'intrattenimento
entrance l'entrata
envelope la busta
equipment l'attrezzatura
escalators le scale mobili
estate car [BE] la station wagon
e-ticket il biglietto elettronico
EU resident il residente UE

euro l'euro

evening la sera

excess l'eccesso

exchange v (money) cambiare;
~ n (place) il cambio;
~ **rate** il tasso di cambio

excursion l'escursione

excuse v scusare

exhausted esausto

exit v uscire; ~ n l'uscita

expensive caro

expert esperto

exposure (film) la posa

express espresso; ~ **bus** il bus
espresso; ~ **train** il treno espresso

extension (phone) l'interno

extra extra; ~ **large** extra large

extract v (tooth) estrarre

eye l'occhio

eyebrow wax la ceretta per
sopracciglie

F

face il viso

facial la pulizia del viso

family la famiglia

fan (appliance) il ventilatore;
~ **(souvenir)** il ventaglio

far lontano; ~-**sighted**
ipermetrope

farm la fattoria

fast veloce; ~ **food** il fast food

faster più veloce

fat free senza grassi

father il padre

fax v inviare per fax; ~ n il fax;
~ **number** il numero di fax

fee la tariffa

feed v dare da mangiare

ferry il traghetto

fever la febbre

field (sports) il campo

fill v riempire; ~ **out** v
(**form**) compilare; ~**ing**
(**tooth**) l'otturazione

film (camera) il rullino

fine (fee for breaking law)
la multa

finger il dito; ~**nail** l'unghia

fire il fuoco; ~ **department** i vigili
del fuoco; ~ **door** la porta
antincendio

first primo; ~ **class** la prima classe

fit (clothing) v andare bene

fitting room il camerino

fix v (repair) riparare

flashlight la torcia elettrica

flat tire la gomma a terra

flight il volo

floor il pavimento

flower il fiore

folk music la musica folk

food il cibo
foot il piede
football game [BE] la partita di football
for per
forecast la previsione
forest il bosco
fork la forchetta
form il modulo
formula (baby) il latte in polvere
fort la fortezza
fountain la fontana
free libero
freezer il freezer
fresh fresco
friend l'amico
frying pan la padella
full-service il servizio completo
full-time a tempo pieno

G

game la partita
garage il garage
garbage bag il sacchetto per la spazzatura
gas (cooking) il gas per cucina; ~ **(heating)** il gas; ~ **station** la stazione del servizio; ~ **(vehicle)** la benzina
gate (airport) l'uscita
gay gay; ~ **bar** il bar per gay; ~ **club** il club per gay
gel (hair) il gel
get off v **(a train/bus/subway)** scendere
get to v arrivare
gift il regalo; ~ **shop** il negozio di articoli da regalo
girl la ragazza; ~**friend** la ragazza
give v dare
glass (drinking) il bicchiere; ~ **(material)** il vetro; ~**es** gli occhiali
go v **(somewhere)** andare
gold l'oro
golf golf; ~ **course** il campo da golf; ~ **club** la mazza; ~ **tournament** la gara di golf
good n il bene; ~ adj buono; ~ **afternoon** buon pomeriggio; ~ **evening** buonasera; ~ **morning** buongiorno; ~ **bye** arrivederla; ~**s** le merci
gram il grammo
grandchild il nipote
grandparent il nonno
gray grigio
green verde
grocery store il fruttivendolo
ground floor il pianterreno
groundcloth [groundsheet BE**]** il telone impermeabile

group il gruppo
guide la guida; ~ **book** la guida;
~ **dog** il cane da guida
gym la palestra
gynecologist il ginecologo

H

hair i capelli; ~ **dryer**
l'asciugacapelli; ~ **salon** il
parrucchiere; ~**brush** la spazzola
; ~ **cut** il taglio; ~**spray** la lacca;
~**style** l'acconciatura; ~**stylist** il
parrucchiere
half la metà; ~ **hour** la mezz'ora;
~**-kilo** il mezzo chilo
hammer il martello
hand la mano; ~ **luggage** il
bagaglio a mano; ~**bag** la
borsetta
handicapped il disabile;
~ **accessible** accessibile ai disabili
hangover la sbornia
happy felice
hat il cappello
have v avere
head (body part) la testa;
~**ache** il mal di testa;
~**phones** gli auricolari
health la salute; ~ **food**
store l'erboristeria
heart il cuore; ~ **condition**
il disturbo cardiaco
heat il calore; ~**er** il radiatore
hello salve
helmet il casco
help v aiutare; ~ n l'aiuto
here qui
heterosexual eterosessuale
hi ciao
high alto; ~**chair** il seggiolone;
~**-heeled shoes** le scarpe col
tacco alto; ~**way** l'autostrada
hiking boots gli scarponi da
montagna
hill la collina
hire v [BE] noleggiare;
~ **car** [BE] l'auto a noleggio
hitchhike v fare l'autostop
hockey l'hockey
holiday [BE] la vacanza
horse track l'ippodromo
hospital l'ospedale
hostel l'ostello
hot (temperature) caldo;
~ **(spicy)** piccante;
~ **springs** le terme;
~ **water** l'acqua calda
hotel l'hotel
hour l'ora
house la casa; ~**hold goods**
gli articoli casalinghi; ~**keeping**
services i servizi di pulizia

domestica
how come; ~ **much** quanto
hug v abbracciare
hungry affamato
hurt il dolore
husband il marito

I

ibuprofen l'ibuprofene
ice il ghiaccio; ~ **hockey** l'hockey su ghiaccio
icy gelato
identification l'identificazione
ill malato
in in
include v includere
indoor pool la piscina interna
inexpensive a buon mercato
infected infetto
information (phone) le informazioni; ~ **desk** l'ufficio informazioni
insect insetto; ~ **bite** la puntura d'insetto; ~ **repellent** il repellente per gli insetti
insert v inserire
insomnia l'insonnia
instant message il messaggio istantaneo
insulin l'insulina
insurance l'assicurazione; ~ **card**

la tessera dell'assicurazione; ~ **company** la compagnia di assicurazione
interesting interessante
intermediate intermedio
international (airport area) internazionale; ~ **flight** il volo internazionale; ~ **student card** la tessera internazionale dello studente
internet l'Internet; ~ **cafe** l'Internet caffè; ~ **service** il servizio Internet; **wireless** ~ il collegamento wireless a Internet
interpreter l'interprete
intersection l'incrocio
intestine l'intestino
introduce v presentare
invoice [BE] la fattura
Ireland l'Irlanda
Irish irlandese
iron v stirare; ~ n (**clothes**) il ferro da stiro
Italian italiano
Italy l'Italia

J

jacket la giacca
jar il vaso
jaw la mascella
jazz il jazz; ~ **club** il club jazz

jeans i jeans
jet ski l'acquascooter
jeweler il gioielliere
jewelry la gioielleria
join v unire
joint (body part) la giuntura

K

key la chiave; ~ **card** la chiave elettronica; ~ **ring** il portachiavi
kiddie pool la piscina per bambini
kidney (body part) il rene
kilo il chilo; ~**gram** il chilogrammo; ~**meter** il chilometro
kiss v baciare
kitchen la cucina; ~ **foil** la carta stagnola
knee il ginocchio
knife il coltello

L

lace il pizzo
lactose intolerant intollerante al lattosio
lake il lago
large grande
larger più grande
last ultimo
late (time) tardi
later più tardi

launderette [BE] la lavanderia a gettone
laundromat la lavanderia a gettone
laundry la lavanderia;
~ **facility** il locale lavanderia;
~ **service** il servizio di lavanderia
lawyer l'avvocato
leather la pelle
leave v partire
left (direction) a sinistra
leg la gamba
lens la lente
less meno
lesson la lezione
letter la lettera
library la biblioteca
life la vita; ~ **jacket** il giubbotto di salvataggio; ~**guard** il bagnino
lift (ride) il passaggio; ~ **[BE]** l'ascensore; ~ **pass** il lift pass
light (overhead) la lampada;
~ v (**cigarette**) accendere;
~**bulb** la lampadina;
~**er** l'accendino
like v (**someone**) piacere
line (train) la linea
linen il lino
lip il labbro
liquor store l'enoteca
liter il litro
little piccolo

live v vivere
liver (body part) il fegato
loafers i mocassini
local locale
lock v chiudere; ~ n la serratura
locker l'armadietto
log off v **(computer)** fare il logoff
log on v **(computer)** fare il logon
long lungo; ~ **sleeves** le
   maniche lunghe; ~-**sighted**
   [BE] ipermetrope
look v guardare
lose v **(something)** perdere
lost perso; ~ **and found** l'ufficio
   oggetti smarriti
lotion la lozione
louder più forte
love v **(someone)** amare; ~ n
   l'amore
low basso; ~**er** più basso
luggage il bagaglio;
   ~ **cart** il carrello bagagli;
   ~ **locker** l'armadietto dei bagagli;
   ~ **ticket** lo scontrino dei bagagli;
   hand ~ [BE] il bagaglio a mano
lunch il pranzo
lung il polmone

M

magazine la rivista
magnificent magnifico

mail v spedire; ~ n la posta;
   ~**box** la cassetta della posta
main principale; ~ **attraction**
   l'attrattiva principale; ~ **course**
   il piatto principale
make up [BE] **(a prescription)**
   il trucco
mall il centro commerciale
man l'uomo
manager il responsabile
manicure il manicure
manual car l'auto col cambio
   manuale
map la cartina
market il mercato
married sposato
marry v sposare
mass (church service) la messa
massage il massaggio
match n **(wooden**
   stick) il fiammifero; ~ n
   (game) la partita
meal il pasto
measure v **(someone/**
   something) misurare; ~**ing**
   cup la tazza di misurazione; ~**ing**
   spoon il misurino
mechanic il meccanico
medicine la medicina
medium (size) medio
meet v **(someone)** incontrare

meeting (corporate) la riunione;
~ **room** sala riunioni
membership card la tessera
associativa
memorial (place) il monumento
memory card la scheda memoria
mend v riparare
menstrual cramp il crampo
mestruale
menu il menù
message il messaggio
meter (parking) il parchimetro
microwave il microonde
midday [BE] mezzogiorno
midnight mezzanotte
mileage il chilometraggio
mini-bar il minibar
minute il minuto
missing (was never there)
mancante; scomparso **(was
previously there)**
mistake l'errore
mobile mobile; ~ **home** la casa
prefabbricata; ~ **phone [BE]** il
telefonino
mobility la mobilità
money il denaro
month il mese
mop lo spazzolone
moped lo scooter
more più

morning il mattino
mosque la moschea
mother la madre
motor il motore; ~ **boat** il
motoscafo; ~**cycle** la motocicletta;
~**way [BE]** l'autostrada
mountain la montagna; ~ **bike** la
mountain bike
mousse (hair) la mousse
mouth la bocca
movie il film; ~ **theater** il cinema
mug v scippare
muscle il muscolo
museum il museo
music la musica; ~ **store** il
negozio di musica

N

nail l'unghia; ~ **file** la lima;
~ **salon** il salone di bellezza
name il nome
napkin il tovagliolo
nappy [BE] il pannolino
nationality la nazionalità
nature preserve la riserva naturale
(be) nauseous v avere la nausea
near vicino; ~-**sighted** miope
neck il collo; ~**lace** la collana
need v necessitare
newspaper il giornale
newsstand l'edicola

next prossimo
nice sympatico
night la notte; ~**club** il nightclub
no no
non-alcoholic analcolico
non-smoking non fumatori
noon mezzogiorno
north nord
nose il naso
notes [BE] le banconote
nothing niente
notify *v* avvertire
novice il principiante
now ora
number il numero
nurse l'infermiere

O

office l'ufficio; ~ **hours** l'orario
  d'ufficio
off-licence [BE] l'enoteca
oil l'olio
OK OK
old vecchio
on the corner all'angolo
once una volta
one uno; ~**-way (ticket)** solo
  andata; ~**-way street** il senso unico
only solo
open *v* aprire; ~ *adj* aperto
opera l'opera; ~ **house** il teatro
  dell'opera
opposite di fronte a
optician l'ottico
orange (color) arancione
orchestra l'orchestra
order *v* ordinare
outdoor pool la piscina esterna
outside fuori
over sopra; ~ **the counter**
  (medication) da banco; ~**look**
  (scenic place) il belvedere;
  ~**night** per la notte
oxygen treatment
  l'ossigeno terapia

P

p.m. del pomeriggio
pacifier il ciuccio
pack *v* fare le valigie
package il pacchetto
paddling pool [BE] la piscina per
  bambini
pad [BE] l'assorbente
pain il dolore
pajamas il pigiama
palace il palazzo
pants i pantaloni
pantyhose il collant
paper la carta; ~ **towel** la carta
  da cucina
paracetamol [BE] il paracetamolo

park *v* parcheggiare; ~ *n* il parco;
  ~ing garage il parcheggio; **~ing
  lot** il parcheggio
parliament building l'edificio del
  parlamento
part (for car) il ricambio;
  ~ time part-time
pass through *v* passare
passenger il passeggero
passport il passaporto;
  ~ control il controllo passaporti
password la password
pastry shop la pasticceria
path il sentiero
pay *v* pagare; **~ phone** il telefono
  pubblico
peak (of a mountain) la vetta
pearl la perla
pedestrian il pedone
pediatrician il pediatra
pedicure il pedicure
pen la penna
penicillin la penicillina
per per; **~ day** al giorno;
  ~ hour all'ora; **~ night** a notte;
  ~ week a settimana
perfume il profumo
period (menstrual) il ciclo;
  ~ (of time) il periodo
permit *v* permettere
petite piccolo

petrol [BE] la benzina; **~ station
  [BE]** la stazione di servizio
pewter il peltro
pharmacy la farmacia
phone *v* telefonare; ~ *n*
  il telefono; **~ call** la telefonata;
  ~ card la scheda telefonica;
  ~ number il numero di telefono
photo la foto; **~copy** la fotocopia;
  ~graphy la fotografia
pick up *v* **(something)** raccogliere
picnic area la zona picnic
piece il pezzo
Pill (birth control) la pillola
pillow il cuscino
**personal identification number
  (PIN)** il codice PIN
pink rosa
piste [BE] la pista; **~ map [BE]** la
  cartina delle piste
pizzeria la pizzeria
place a bet *v* scommettere
plane l'aereo
plastic wrap la pellicola per
  alimenti
plate il piatto
platform (train) il binario
platinum il platino
play *v* giocare; **~** *n* **(theater)**
  lo spettacolo; **~ ground** il parco
  giochi; **~ pen** il box

please per favore
pleasure il piacere
plunger lo sturalavandini
plus size la taglia forte
pocket la tasca
poison il veleno
poles (skiing) le racchette
police la polizia; **~ report**
il verbale di polizia; **~ station**
il commissariato
pond lo stagno
pool (swimming) la piscina
pop music la musica pop
portion la porzione
post [BE] la posta; **~ office**
l'ufficio postale; **~box [BE]**
la buca delle lettere; **~card**
la cartolina
pot (for cooking) la pentola;
~ (for flowers) il vaso
pottery la ceramica
pounds (British sterling)
le sterline
pregnant incinta
prescribe v prescrivere
prescription la ricetta
press v (**clothing**) stirare
price il prezzo
print v stampare
problem il problema
produce la frutta e verdura;

~ store il fruttivendolo
prohibit v proibire
pronounce v pronunciare
public pubblico
pull v (**door sign**) tirare
purple viola
purse la borsetta
push v (**door sign**) spingere;
~chair [BE] il passeggino

Q

quality la qualità
question la domanda
quiet tranquillo

R

racetrack il circuito
racket (sports) la racchetta
railway station [BE] la stazione
ferroviaria
rain la pioggia; **~coat**
l'impermeabile; **~forest** la foresta
pluviale; **~y** piovoso
rape v stuprare; **~** n lo stupro
rash l'irritazione
razor blade la lametta
reach v raggiungere
ready pronto
real vero
receipt la ricevuta
receive v ricevere

reception la reception
recharge v ricaricare
recommend v raccomandare
recommendation la raccomandazione
recycling il reciclaggio
red rosso
refrigerator il frigorifero
region la regione
registered mail la raccomandata
regular normale
relationship la relazione
rent v affittare
rental car l'auto a noleggio
repair v riparare
repeat v ripetere
reservation la prenotazione; ~ **desk** l'ufficio prenotazioni
reserve v prenotare
restaurant il ristorante
restroom la toilette
retired in pensione
return v (something) portare indietro; ~ n [BE] la resa
rib (body part) la costola
right (direction) a destra; ~ **of way** la precedenza
ring l'anello
river il fiume
road map la cartina stradale
rob v rubare; ~bed derubato

romantic romantico
room la stanza; ~ **key** la chiave della stanza; ~ **service** il servizio in camera
round-trip l'andata e ritorno
route il percorso
rowboat la barca a remi
rubbish [BE] la spazzatura; ~ **bag** [BE] il sacchetto per la spazzatura
rugby il rugby
ruins le rovine
rush la fretta

S

sad triste
safe (receptacle) la cassaforte; ~ (protected) sicuro
sales tax l'IVA
same stesso
sandals i sandali
sanitary napkin l'assorbente
saucepan la pentola
sauna la sauna
save v (computer) salvare
savings (account) i risparmi
scanner lo scanner
scarf la sciarpa
schedule v programmare; ~ n il programma
school la scuola

science la scienza
scissors le forbici
sea il mare
seat il posto
security la sicurezza
see v vedere
self-service il self-service
sell v vendere
seminar il seminario
send v inviare
senior citizen l'anziano
separated (marriage) separato
serious serio
service (in a restaurant)
  il servizio
**sexually transmitted disease
  (STD)** la malattia sessualmente
  trasmissibile
shampoo lo shampoo
sharp appuntito
shaving cream la crema da barba
sheet (bedlinen) il lenzuolo;
  ~ **(paper)** la pagina
ship v **(mail)** inviare
shirt la camicia
shoes le scarpe; ~ **store** il negozio
  di calzature
shop v fare lo shopping
shopping lo shopping; ~ **area**
  la zona commerciale; ~ **centre**
  [BE] il centro commerciale;

~ **mall** il centro commerciale
short corto; ~ **sleeves** le maniche
  corte; ~**s** i pantaloncini corti;
  ~**-sighted** [BE] miope
shoulder la spalla
show v mostrare
shower la doccia
shrine il santuario
sick malato
side il lato; ~ **dish** il contorno;
  ~ **effect** l'effetto collaterale;
  ~ **order** il contorno
sightseeing la visita turistica;
  ~ **tour** la gita turistica
sign v firmare
silk la seta
silver l'argento
single (marriage) single;
  ~ **bed** il letto a una piazza;
  ~ **prints** le stampe singole;
  ~ **room** la stanza singola
sink il lavandino
sister la sorella
sit v sedersi
size la taglia
skin la pelle
skirt la gonna
ski v sciare; ~ n lo sci; ~ **lift** lo
  ski lift
sleep v dormire; ~**er car** il vagone
  letto; ~**ing bag** il sacco a pelo;

~ing car [BE] il vagone letto
slice (of something) la fetta
slippers le ciabatte
slow lento; **~er** più lento;
  ~ly lentamente
small piccolo; **~er** più piccolo
smoke v fumare
smoking (area) per fumatori
snack bar lo snack bar
sneakers le scarpe da ginnastica
snorkeling equipment
  l'attrezzatura da immersione
snow neve; **~board** lo snowboard;
  ~shoe la scarpa da neve;
  ~y nevoso
soap il sapone
soccer il calcio
sock il calzino
some qualche
soother [BE] il ciuccio
sore throat il mal di gola
sorry scusi
south sud
souvenir il souvenir; **~ store** il
  negozio di souvenir
spa la stazione termale
spatula la spatola
speak v parlare
special (food) la specialità; **~ist**
  (doctor) lo specialista
specimen il campione

speeding l'eccesso di velocità
spell v scrivere
spicy piccante
spine (body part) la spina
  dorsale
spoon il cucchiaio
sport lo sport; **~s**
  massage il massaggio sportivo
sporting goods store il negozio di
  articoli sportivi
sprain la storta
square quadrato; **~**
  kilometer il chilometro quadrato;
  ~ meter il metro quadrato
stadium lo stadio
stairs le scale
stamp v **(a ticket)** convalidare;
  ~ n **(postage)** il francobollo
start v iniziare
starter [BE] lo starter
station la stazione; **bus ~** la
  stazione dei bus; **gas ~** il
  benzinaio; **petrol ~ [BE]** il
  benzinaio; **railway ~ [BE]** la
  stazione ferroviaria; **subway**
  ~ la stazione della metropolitana
  train ~ la stazione ferroviaria;
  underground ~ [BE] la stazione
  della metropolitana;
  ~ wagon la station wagon
statue la statua

stay v stare

steal v rubare

steep ripido

sterling silver l'argento massiccio

sting la puntura

stolen rubato

stomach lo stomaco; **~ache** il mal di stomaco

stop v fermarsi; **~** n la fermata

store directory la piantina del negozio

storey [BE] il piano

stove la cucina

straight dritto

strange strano

stream il ruscello

stroller il passeggino

student lo studente

study v studiare

stunning fenomenale

subtitle il sottotitolo

subway la metropolitana; **~ station** la stazione della metropolitana

suit l'abito; **~case** la valigia

sun il sole; **~block** il filtro solare; **~burn** la scottatura; **~glasses** gli occhiali da sole; **~ny** soleggiato; **~screen** il filtro solare; **~stroke** l'insolazione

super (fuel) la super; **~market** il supermercato; **~vision** la supervisione

surfboard la tavola da surf

swallow v ingoiare

sweater il maglione

sweatshirt la felpa

sweet (taste) dolce; **~s** [BE] le caramelle

swelling il gonfiore

swim v nuotare; **~suit** il costume da bagno

symbol (keyboard) il simbolo

synagogue la sinagoga

T

table il tavolo

tablet (medicine) la compressa

take v prendere; **~ away** [BE] portare via

tampon il tampone

taste v assaggiare

taxi il taxi

team la squadra

teaspoon il cucchiaino

telephone il telefono

temple (religious) il tempio

temporary provvisorio

tennis il tennis

tent la tenda; **~ peg** il picchetto da tenda; **~ pole** il paletto da tenda

terminal (airport) il terminal
terracotta la terracotta
terrible terribile
text v **(send a message)** inviare SMS; ~ n **(message)** il testo
thank v ringraziare; ~ **you** grazie
that che
theater il teatro
theft il furto
there là
thief il ladro
thirsty assetato
this questo
throat la gola
ticket il biglietto; ~ **office** la biglietteria; ~**ed passenger** il passeggero con biglietto
tie (clothing) la cravatta
time il tempo; ~**table** [BE] l'orario
tire lo pneumatico
tired stanco
tissue il fazzoletto di carta
tobacconist il tabaccaio
today oggi
toe il dito del piede; ~**nail** l'unghia
toilet [BE] la toilette; ~ **paper** la carta igienica
tomorrow domani
tongue la lingua
tonight stanotte

too troppo
tooth il dente; ~**paste** il dentifricio
total (amount) il totale
tough (food) duro
tourist il turista; ~ **information office** l'ufficio informazioni turistiche
tour la gita
tow truck il carro attrezzi
towel l'asciugamano
tower la torre
town la città; ~ **hall** il municipio; ~ **map** la cartina della città; ~ **square** la piazza della città
toy il giocattolo; ~ **store** il negozio di giocattoli
track (train) il binario
traditional tradizionale
traffic light il semaforo
trail il sentiero; ~ **map** la mappa dei sentieri
trailer la roulotte
train il treno; ~ **station** la stazione ferroviaria
transfer v **(change trains/flights)** cambiare; ~ v **(money)** trasferire
translate v tradurre
trash la spazzatura
travel viaggiare; ~ **agency** l'agenzia viaggi; ~ **sickness**

(air) il mal d'aria; ~ **sickness**
(car) il mal d'auto; ~ **sickness**
(sea) il mal di mare; ~**ers**
tree l'albero
trim (hair) una spuntatina
trip il viaggio
trolley [BE] il carrello
trousers i pantaloni
T-shirt la maglietta
turn off v spegnere
turn on v accendere
TV la TV
type v battere a macchina
tyre [BE] lo pneumatico

U

United Kingdom (U.K.) il Regno Unito
United States (U.S.) gli Stati Uniti
ugly brutto
umbrella l'ombrello
unattended incustodito
unconscious inconscio
underground [BE]
la metropolitana; ~ **station [BE]** la stazione della metropolitana
underpants le mutande
understand v capire
underwear la biancheria intima
university l'università
unleaded (gas) senza piombo

upper superiore
upset stomach lo stomaco in disordine
urgent urgente
use v usare
username il nome utente

V

vacancy la disponibilità
vacation la vacanza
vaccination la vaccinazione
vacuum cleaner l'aspirapolvere
vaginal infection l'infezione vaginale
valid valido
valley la valle
valuable di valore
value il valore
VAT [BE] l'IVA
vegetarian vegetariano
vehicle registration il numero di targa
viewpoint la prospettiva
village il villaggio
vineyard il vigneto
visa il visto
visit v visitare;
~**ing hours** gli orari di visita
visually impaired ipovedente
volleyball game la partita di pallavolo
vomit v vomitare

W

wait *v* attendere; ~ *n* l'attesa;
~**ing room** la sala d'attesa
waiter il cameriere
waitress la cameriera
wake *v* svegliare, svegliarsi;
~**-up call** il servizio sveglia
walk *v* camminare; ~ *n* la
passeggiata; ~**ing route** il
percorso pedonale
wallet il portafogli
warm *v* (**something**) riscaldare;
~ *adj* (**temperature**) caldo
washing machine la lavatrice
watch l'orologio
water skis lo sci d'acqua
waterfall la cascata
weather il tempo
week la settimana;
~**end** il fine settimana;
~**ly** settimanalmente
welcome *v* accogliere
west ovest
what (question) cosa
wheelchair la sedia a rotelle; ~
ramp la rampa per sedia a rotelle
when (question) quando
where (question) dove
white bianco; ~ **gold** l'oro bianco
who (question) chi
widowed vedovo

wife la moglie
window la finestra; ~ **case** la
vetrina
windsurfer il windsurf
wine list la carta dei vini
wireless wireless; ~ **internet**
l'Internet wireless; ~ **internet**
service il servizio Internet wireless;
~ **phone** il telefono cordless
with con
withdraw *v* ritirare; ~**al (bank)**
il prelievo
without senza
woman la donna
wool la lana
work *v* lavorare
wrap *v* incartare
wrist il polso
write *v* scrivere

Y

year l'anno
yellow giallo; ~ **gold** l'oro giallo
yes sì
yesterday ieri
young giovane
youth hostel l'ostello della gioventù

Z

zoo lo zoo

Italian–English

A

a buon mercato inexpensive
a destra right (direction)
a girocollo crew neck
a notte per night
a settimana per week
a sinistra left (direction)
a tempo pieno full-time
l'abbazia abbey
l'abbigliamento clothing
abbracciare to hug
l'abito suit
accendere v light (cigarette); ~ v turn on (lights)
l'accendino lighter
accessibile ai disabili handicapped- [disabled BE] accessible
l'accesso access
accettare v accept
accogliere v welcome
l'acconciatura hairstyle
l'acconto cash advance
l'acqua water; ~ **calda** hot water; ~ **potabile** drinking water; ~**scooter** jet ski
l'adattatore adapter
addebitare v charge (credit card)
l'aereo airplane

l'aeroporto airport
affamato hungry
affittare v rent [hire BE]
l'agenzia agency; ~ **viaggi** travel agency
l'aggressione attack (on person)
l'agopuntura acupuncture
l'AIDS AIDS
aiutare to help
l'aiuto n help
al giorno per day
l'albero tree
all'angolo on the corner
allattare breastfeed
allergico allergic
l'alloggio accommodation
all'ora per hour
alto high
amare v love (someone)
l'ambulanza ambulance
americano American
l'amico friend
l'amore n love
analcolico non-alcoholic
andare v go (somewhere); ~ **bene** fit (clothing)
l'andata e ritorno round-trip
l'anello ring
anemico anemic

l'anestesia anesthesia
l'animale animal
l'anno year
annullare v cancel
l'antibiotico antibiotic
l'antipasto appetizer [starter BE]
l'anziano senior citizen
aperto adj open
l'appartamento apartment
l'appendice appendix (body part)
l'appuntamento appointment
appuntito sharp
l'apribottiglie bottle opener
aprire v open
l'apriscatole can opener
arancione orange (color)
l'argento silver; ~ **massiccio**
  sterling silver
l'aria condizionata air
  conditioning
l'armadietto locker; ~ **dei bagagli**
  luggage locker
l'aromaterapia aromatherapy
arrivare v arrive
arrivederla goodbye
gli arrivi arrivals (airport)
l'arte art
l'arteria artery
gli articoli casalinghi household
  goods
l'artrite arthritis

l'ascensore elevator
l'asciugacapelli hair dryer
l'asciugamano towel
asmatico asthmatic
l'aspirapolvere vacuum cleaner
l'aspirina aspirin
assaggiare v taste
l'assegno n check (payment)
  [cheque BE]
assetato thirsty
l'assicurazione insurance
l'assorbente sanitary napkin
  [pad BE]
**l'astuccio della macchina
  fotografica** camera case
attendere v wait
l'attesa n wait
attraente attractive
l'attrattiva attraction (place);
  ~ **principale** main attraction
l'attrezzatura equipment;
  ~ **da immersione** snorkeling
  equipment; ~ **subacquea** diving
  equipment
gli auricolari headphones
Australia Australia
australiano Australian
l'auto car; ~**bus** bus; ~ **con il
  cambio automatico** automatic
  car; ~ **con il cambio manuale**
  manual car; ~ **a noleggio** rental

[hire BE] car
automatico automatic
l'autonoleggio car rental [hire BE]
l'autostrada highway
[motorway BE]
avere v have; ~ **la nausea** v
be nauseous
avvertire v notify
l'avvocato lawyer

B

la babysitter babysitter
baciare v kiss
il bagaglio luggage [baggage
BE]; ~ **a mano** carry-on [hand
luggage BE]
il bagnino lifeguard
il bagno bathroom
ballare v dance
il ballo dancing
il balsamo conditioner
il bambino child
la bambola doll
la banca bank
il bancomat ATM, ATM card, debit
card
la banconota n bill (money)
[note BE]
il bar bar; ~ **per gay** gay bar
il barbecue barbecue
il barbiere barber

la barca boat; ~ **a remi** rowboat
il baseball baseball
il basketball basketball
basso low
i bastoncini cinesi chopsticks
battere a macchina v type
la batteria battery
il bebè baby
beige beige
bello beautiful
il belvedere overlook (scenic place)
ben riposato well-rested
la benda bandage
bene good
la benzina gas (vehicle) [petrol BE]
il benzinaio gas [petrol BE] station
bere v drink
la bevanda n drink
la biancheria intima underwear
bianco white
il biberon baby bottle
la biblioteca library
il bicchiere glass (drinking)
la bicicletta bicycle
la biglietteria ticket office
il biglietto ticket; ~ **del bus** bus
ticket; ~ **elettronico** e-ticket;
~ **da visita** business card
il bikini bikini
il binario platform; track (train)
blu blue

la bocca mouth
la borsa bag
la borsetta purse [handbag BE]
il bosco forest
la bottiglia bottle
il box playpen
il braccialetto bracelet
il braccio arm
bruciare v burn
brutto ugly
la buca delle lettere postbox
buongiorno good morning
buon pomeriggio good afternoon
buonasera good evening
buono adj good
il bus espresso express bus
la busta envelope

C

il cabaret cabaret
la cabina cabin
il caffè cafe, coffee
il calcio soccer
caldo hot (temperature)
il calore heat [heating BE]
le calorie calories
il calzino sock
cambiare v change; ~ v exchange;
  ~ v transfer
il cambio n change (money);
  ~ n exchange (place);

~ valuta currency exchange
la cameriera waitress
il cameriere waiter
la camicetta blouse
la camicia shirt
camminare v walk
campeggiare v camp
il campeggio campsite
il campione specimen
il campo field (sports);
  ~ da golf golf course;
  ~ di battaglia battleground
il Canada Canada
canadese Canadian
il canalone canyon
cancellare v clear (on an ATM)
il cane da guida guide dog
i capelli hair
capire v understand
il cappello hat
il cappotto coat
la caraffa carafe
le caramelle candy [sweet BE]
il carbone charcoal
carino cute
caro expensive
il carrello cart [trolley BE];
  ~ bagagli luggage cart
il carro attrezzi tow truck
la carta card, paper;
  ~ di credito credit card;

~ da cucina paper towel;
~ igienica toilet paper;
~ d'imbarco boarding pass;
~ stagnola aluminum [kitchen BE] foil; **~ dei vini** wine list
la cartina map; **~ della città** town map; **~ delle piste** trail [piste BE] map; **~ stradale** road map
la cartolina postcard
il cartone carton
la casa house
la cascata waterfall
il casco helmet
il casinò casino
la cassa case (container); **~forte** safe (for valuables)
la cassetta della posta mailbox
il cassiere cashier
il castello castle
la cattedrale cathedral
il cavatappi corkscrew
la caviglia ankle
il CD CD
Celsius Celsius
la cena dinner
il centimetro centimeter
il centro downtown area; **~ business** business center; **~ commerciale** shopping mall [centre BE]

la ceramica pottery
la ceretta wax; **~ all'inguine** bikini wax; **~ per sopracciglie** eyebrow wax
il certificato certificate
il cestino basket (grocery store)
che that
il check-in check-in (hotel/airport)
chi who
chiamare v call
la chiamata n call
la chiave key; **~ elettronica** key card; **~ della stanza** room key
la chiesa church
il chilo kilo; **~grammo** kilogram; **~metraggio** mileage; **~metro** kilometer; **~metro quadrato** square kilometer
chiudere v close (a shop); **~** v lock
chiuso closed
le ciabatte slippers
ciao hi, bye
il cibo food
il ciclismo cycling
il ciclo period (menstrual)
il cinema movie theater
cinese Chinese
la cintura belt
il circuito racetrack
la città town
il ciuccio pacifier [soother BE]

la classe class; ~ **business** business class; ~ **economica** economy class

il club club; ~ **di ballo** dance club; ~ **jazz** jazz club; ~ **per gay** gay club

il codice code; ~ **di abbigliamento** dress code; ~ **PIN** personal identification number (PIN)

la coincidenza connection (flight)

la colazione breakfast

la collana necklace

il collant pantyhose

il collega colleague

il collegamento connection (internet); ~ **wireless a Internet** wireless internet

collegarsi v connect (internet)

la collina hill

il collo neck

la colonia cologne

il colore color

il coltello knife

come how

il commissariato police station

la compagnia aerea airline

la compagnia di assicurazione insurance company

compilare v fill out (form)

il compleanno birthday

comporre il numero v dial

comprare v buy

la compressa tablet (medicine)

il computer computer

con with

il concerto concert

la condizione condition (medical)

la conferenza conference

confermare v confirm

la congestione congestion

il consolato consulate

il consulente consultant

contagioso contagious

i contanti n cash

contattare to contact

il conto n bill (of sale); ~ account; ~ **corrente** checking [current BE] account

il contorno side dish

controllare v check (luggage)

il controllo passaporti passport control

convalidare v stamp (a ticket)

la coperta blanket

il coperto cover charge

la coppa bowl

il corridoio aisle

corto short

cosa what (question)

la coscia thigh

costare v cost

costipato constipated
il costo charge (cost)
la costola rib (body part)
il costume da bagno swimsuit
il cotone cotton
il crampo mestruale menstrual cramp
la cravatta tie (clothing)
la crema cream (ointment);
~ **antisettica** antiseptic cream;
~ **da barba** shaving cream
il cristallo crystal
la cuccetta berth
il cucchiaino teaspoon
il cucchiaio spoon
la cucina kitchen, stove
cucinare v cook
la culla crib
il cuore heart
il cuscino pillow

D

da banco over the counter (medication)
danneggiare v damage
danneggiato damaged
dare v give; ~ **da mangiare** v feed
la data date (calendar)
del pomeriggio p.m.
il denaro money

il dente tooth
la dentiera denture
il dentifricio toothpaste
il dentista dentist
il deodorante deodorant
depositare v deposit
il deposito n deposit
derubato robbed
il deserto desert
il detersivo detergent;
~ **per i piatti** dishwashing liquid
di fronte a opposite
di valore valuable
diabetico diabetic
il diamante diamond
la diarrea diarrhea
dichiarare v declare
il diesel diesel
dietro around (the corner), behind (direction)
difficile difficult
digitale digital
la direzione direction
il disabile handicapped [disabled BE]
la disponibilità vacancy
il disturbo cardiaco heart condition
il dito finger; ~ **del piede** toe
divorziare v divorce
la doccia shower

la dogana customs
dolce sweet (taste)
il dollaro dollar (U.S.)
il dolore hurt (pain);
~ **al petto** chest pain
la domanda question
domani tomorrow
domestico domestic
la donna woman
dopo after; ~**barba** aftershave
doppiato dubbed
dormire v sleep
il dormitorio dormitory
dove where (question)
la dozzina dozen
dritto straight
durante during
duro tough (food)
duty-free duty-free
il DVD DVD

E

e and
l'eccesso excess; ~ **di velocità**
speeding
economico cheap
l'edicola newsstand
l'edificio building; ~ **del**
parlamento parliament building
l'effetto collaterale side effect
eliminare v delete (computer)

l'e-mail n e-mail
l'emergenza emergency
l'enoteca liquor store [off-licence
BE]
entrare v enter
l'entrata entrance
l'erboristeria health food store
l'errore mistake
esausto exhausted
l'escursione excursion;
~ **in pullman** bus tour
esperto expert
espresso express
essere v be
est east
estrarre v extract (tooth)
l'età age
l'euro euro
extra extra; ~ **large** extra large

F

facile easy
la famiglia family
fare v do; ~ **l'autostop**
v hitchhike; ~ **la ceretta** v wax;
~ **un incidente** v crash (car);
~ **il logoff** v log off (computer);
~ **il logon** v log on (computer);
~ **lo shopping** v shop;
~ **le valigie** v pack
la farmacia pharmacy [chemist BE]

il fast food fast food
la fattoria farm
la fattura bill [invoice BE]
fatturare v bill (charge)
il fax n fax
il fazzoletto di carta tissue
la febbre fever
il fegato liver (body part)
felice happy
la felpa sweatshirt
fenomenale stunning
fermarsi v stop
la fermata n stop; ~ **del bus** bus stop
il ferro da stiro n iron (clothes)
la fetta slice (of something)
il fiammifero n match (wooden stick)
il film movie
il filtro solare sunblock, sunscreen
il fine settimana weekend
la finestra window
finire v end
il fiore flower
firmare v sign
il fiume river
la fontana fountain
le forbici scissors
la forchetta fork
la foresta pluviale rainforest
il fornello da campeggio camping stove
la fortezza fort
la foto photo; ~ **digitale** digital photo; ~**copia** photocopy; ~**grafia** photography
il francobollo n stamp (postage)
il fratello brother
freddo cold (temperature)
il freezer freezer
i freni brakes (car)
frequentare to attend
fresco cool (temperature); ~ fresh
la fretta rush
il frigorifero refrigerator
la frutta e verdura produce
il fruttivendolo grocery store
fumare v smoke
la funivia cable car
il fuoco fire
fuori outside
il furto theft; ~ **con scasso** break-in (burglary)

G

la gamba leg
la gara di golf golf tournament
il garage garage
il gas gas (heating); ~ **per cucina** cooking gas
la gastronomia delicatessen
gay gay

il gel gel (hair)
gelato icy
il ghiaccio ice
la giacca jacket
giallo yellow
il giardino botanico botanical garden
il ginecologo gynecologist
il ginocchio knee
giocare v play
il giocattolo toy
la gioielleria jewelry
il gioielliere jeweler
il giornale newspaper
il giorno day
giovane young
la gita tour; ~ **turistica** sightseeing tour
il giubbotto di salvataggio life jacket
la giuntura joint (body part)
la goccia drop (medicine)
godersi v enjoy
la gola throat
il gomito elbow
la gomma rubber; ~ **a terra** flat tire; ~ **da masticare** chewing gum
il gonfiore swelling
la gonna skirt
i gradi degrees (temperature)

il grammo gram
grande big, large; ~ **magazzino** department store
grazie thank you
grigio gray
la grotta cave
il gruppo group
guardare v look
il guasto breakdown
la guida guide, guide book
guidare v drive

H

l'hockey hockey; ~ **su ghiaccio** ice hockey
l'hotel hotel

I

l'ibuprofene ibuprofen
l'identificazione identification
ieri yesterday
imbarcarsi v board
l'impermeabile raincoat
in in; ~ **pensione** retired
incartare v wrap
incassare v cash
l'incidente accident
incidere v engrave
incinta pregnant
includere v include
inconscio unconscious

incontrare *v* meet (someone)
l'incontro di boxe boxing match
l'incrocio intersection
incustodito unattended
l'indirizzo address;
~ **e-mail** e-mail address
infastidire *v* bother
l'infermiere nurse
infetto infected
l'infezione vaginale vaginal
infection
le informazioni information
(phone)
inglese English
ingoiare *v* swallow
l'ingresso admission
iniziare *v* begin, start
inserire *v* insert
l'insetto bug
insipido bland
l'insolazione sunstroke
l'insonnia insomnia
l'insulina insulin
interessante interesting
intermedio intermediate
internazionale international
(airport area)
l'Internet internet; ~ **caffè**
internet cafe; ~ **wireless** wireless
internet
l'interno extension (phone)

l'interprete interpreter
l'intestino intestine
intollerante al lattosio lactose
intolerant
l'intrattenimento
entertainment
inviare *v* send, ship (mail);
~ **e-mail** *v* e-mail; ~ **per fax**
v fax; ~ **SMS** *v* text (send a
message)
ipermetrope far- [long- BE]
sighted
ipovedente visually impaired
l'ippodromo horsetrack
l'Irlanda Ireland
irlandese Irish
l'irritazione rash
l'Italia Italy
italiano Italian
l'IVA sales tax [VAT BE]

J

il jazz jazz
i jeans jeans

L

là there
la casa prefabbricata mobile hom[e]
la stanza singola single room
il labbro lip
la lacca hairspray

il ladro thief

il lago lake

la lametta razor blade; **~ usa e getta** disposable razor

la lampadina lightbulb

la lana wool

il latte in polvere formula (baby)

il lato side

la lavanderia laundry; **~ a gettone** laundromat [launderette BE]

il lavandino sink

il lavasecco dry cleaner

la lavastoviglie dishwasher

la lavatrice washing machine

lavorare v work

il lavoro business

lentamente slowly

la lente lens; **~ a contatto** contact lens

il lenzuolo sheet

la lettera letter

il lettino cot

il letto bed; **~ matrimoniale** double bed; **~ a una piazza** single bed

la lezione lesson

libero available, free

la libreria bookstore

il libro book

il lift pass lift pass

la lima nail file

la linea line (train)

la lingua tongue

il lino linen

il litro liter

locale local

lontano far

la lozione lotion

la luce light (overhead)

il lunapark amusement park

lungo long

M

la macchina fotografica camera; **~ digitale** digital camera

il macellaio butcher

la madre mother

la maglietta T-shirt

il maglione sweater

magnifico magnificent

il mal sickness; **~ d'aria** motion sickness (air); **~ d'auto** motion sickness (car); **~ di gola** sore throat; **~ di mare** motion sickness (sea); **~ d'orecchio** earache; **~ di schiena** backache; **~ di stomaco** stomachache; **~ di testa** headache

malato sick [ill BE]

malattia sessualmente

trasmissibile sexually transmitted disease (STD)
mancante missing
mangiare *v* eat
le maniche sleeves;
  ~ corte short sleeves;
  ~ lunghe long sleeves
il manicure manicure
la mano hand
il mare sea
il marito husband
marrone brown
il martello hammer
la mascella jaw
il massaggio massage;
  ~ sportivo sports massage
il mattino morning
del mattino a.m.
il meccanico mechanic
la medicina medicine
il medico doctor
medio medium (size)
meno less
il menù menu; **~ delle**
  bevande drink menu; **~ per**
  bambini children's menu
il mercato market
le merci goods
il mese month
la messa mass (church service)
il messaggio message;

~ istantaneo instant message
la metà half
il metro quadrato square meter
la metropolitana subway
  [underground BE]
la mezz'ora half hour
la mezzanotte midnight
il mezzo chilo half-kilo
mezzogiorno noon [midday BE]
il microonde microwave
migliore better
il migliore best
il minibar mini-bar
il minuto minute
miope near- [short- BE] sighted
misurare *v* measure (someone,
  something)
il misurino measuring spoon
mobile mobile
la mobilità mobility
i mocassini loafers
il mocio mop
modificare *v* alter (clothing)
il modulo form (fill-in)
la moglie wife
la moneta coin
la montagna mountain
il monumento memorial (place)
la moschea mosque
mostrare *v* show
la motocicletta motorcycle

il motore motor
il motoscafo motor boat
la mountain bike mountain bike
la mousse mousse (hair)
la multa fine (fee for breaking law)
il municipio town hall
il muscolo muscle
il museo museum
la musica music; **~ classica** classical music; **~ folk** folk music; **~ pop** pop music
le mutande underpants

N

il naso nose
il nastro trasportatore conveyor belt
le natiche buttocks
la nazionalità nationality
necessitare *v* need
il negozio store; **~ d'abbigliamento** clothing store; **~ d'antiquariato** antique store; **~ di articoli da regalo** gift shop; **~ di articoli sportivi** sporting goods store; **~ di calzature** shoe store; **~ di fotografia** camera store; **~ di giocattoli** toy store; **~ di musica** music store; **~ di souvenir** souvenir store

nero black
la neve snow
nevoso snowy
niente nothing
il nightclub nightclub
il nipote grandchild
no no
noioso boring
il nome name; **~ utente** username
non fumatori non-smoking
il nonno grandparent
nord north
normale regular
la notte night
il numero number; **~ di fax** fax number; **~ di patente** driver's license number; **~ di targa** vehicle registration; **~ di telefono** phone number
nuotare *v* swim

O

gli occhiali glasses; **~ da sole** sunglasses
l'occhio eye
oggi today
OK OK
l'olio oil
l'ombrello umbrella
l'opera opera

ora now
l'ora hour
gli orari di visita visiting hours
l'orario schedule [timetable BE];
 ~ d'apertura business hours;
 ~ d'ufficio office hours
l'orchestra orchestra
ordinare v order
gli orecchini earrings
l'orecchio ear
l'oro gold;
 ~bianco white gold;
 ~ giallo yellow gold
l'orologio watch;
 ~ da parete wall clock
l'ospedale hospital
l'osso bone
l'ostello hostel; **~ della
 gioventù** youth hostel
l'ottico optician
l'otturazione filling (tooth)
ovest west

P

il pacchetto package
la padella frying pan
il padre father
il pagamento del conto check-out
 (hotel)
pagare v pay
il palazzo palace

la palestra gym
il paletto da tenda tent pole
la panetteria bakery
il pannolino diaper [nappy BE]
i pantaloncini corti shorts
i pantaloni pants [trousers BE]
il paracetamolo acetaminophen
 [paracetamol BE]
parcheggiare v park
il parcheggio parking garage;
 ~ parking lot [car park BE]
il parco n park; **~ giochi**
 playground
parlare v speak
il parrucchiere hair salon
le partenze departures (airport)
partire v leave
la partita game, match; **~ di
 football** soccer [football game
 BE]; **~ di pallavolo** volleyball
 game
part-time part-time
il passaggio lift
il passaporto passport
passare v pass through
il passeggero passenger; **~ con
 biglietto** ticketed passenger
la passeggiata n walk
il passeggino stroller [pushchair
 BE]
la password password

la pasticceria pastry shop
il pasto meal
il pediatra pediatrician
il pedicure pedicure
il pedone pedestrian
la pelle leather, skin
la pellicola per alimenti plastic wrap [cling film BE]
il peltro pewter
il pene penis
la penicillina penicillin
la penna pen
la pensione bed and breakfast
la pentola saucepan, pot
per for, per; ~ **favore** please; ~ **fumatori** smoking (area); ~ **la notte** overnight
il percorso route; ~ **alternativo** alternate route; ~ **ciclabile** bike route; ~ **pedonale** walking route
perdere v lose (something)
la perdita discharge (bodily fluid)
pericoloso dangerous
il periodo period (of time)
la perla pearl
permettere v allow, permit
perso lost
il pettine comb
il petto chest (body part)
il petto breast

il pezzo piece
piacere v like
il piacere pleasure
il piano floor [storey BE]
il pianterreno ground floor
la piantina del negozio store directory
il piatto plate; ~ **principale** main course
la piazza della città town square
piccante hot (spicy)
il picchetto da tenda tent peg
piccolo little, petite, small
il piede foot
il pigiama pajamas
la pillola Pill (birth control)
la pioggia rain
piovoso rainy
la piscina pool; ~ **per bambini** kiddie [paddling BE] pool; ~ **esterna** outdoor pool; ~ **interna** indoor pool
pista piste [BE]
più more; ~ **basso** lower; ~ **economico** cheaper; ~ **forte** louder; ~ **grande** bigger; ~ **lento** slower; ~ **piccolo** smaller; ~ **tardi** later; ~ **veloce** faster
la pizzeria pizzeria
il pizzo lace
il platino platinum

lo pneumatico tire [tyre BE]
la polizia police
il polmone lung
il polso wrist
il pomeriggio afternoon
la pompa dell'aria air pump
il ponte bridge
la porta door; ~ **antincendio** fire door
il portachiavi key ring
il portafogli wallet
portare v bring; ~ **indietro** v return (something); ~ **via** to go [take away BE]
la porzione portion; ~ **per bambini** children's portion
la posa exposure (film)
la posta n mail [post BE]; ~ **aerea** airmail
il posto seat; ~ **sul corridoio** aisle seat
il pranzo lunch
la precedenza right of way
il prefisso area code; ~ **del paese** country code
il prelievo withdrawal (bank)
prendere v take
prenotare v reserve
la prenotazione reservation
la presa elettrica electric outlet
prescrivere v prescribe

presentare v introduce
il preservativo condom
la pressione sanguigna blood pressure
presto early
la previsione forecast
il prezzo price
prima before, earlier; ~ **classe** first class
primo first
il principiante beginner, novice
il problema problem
i prodotti per la pulizia cleaning supplies
profondamente deeply
il profumo perfume
il programma n schedule
programmare v schedule
proibire v prohibit
pronto ready
pronunciare v pronounce
la prospettiva viewpoint
prossimo next
provvisorio temporary
pubblico public
pulire v clean
pulito adj clean
la pulizia del viso facial
la puntura sting; ~ **d'insetto** insect bite

Q

quadrato square
qualche some
la qualità quality
qualsiasi cosa anything
quando when (question)
quanto how much (question)
questo this
qui here

R

la racchetta racket (sports)
le racchette poles (skiing)
raccogliere v pick up (something)
raccomandare v recommend
la raccomandata registered mail
la raccomandazione
  recommendation
il radiatore heater
il raffreddore cold (sickness)
la ragazza girl, girlfriend
il ragazzo boy, boyfriend
raggiungere v reach (get hold of)
il rame copper
la rampa per sedia a rotelle
  wheelchair ramp
il rap rap (music)
la reazione allergica allergic
  reaction
la reception reception
il reclamo complaint

il regalo gift
il reggiseno bra
la regione region
il Regno Unito United Kingdom
  (U.K.)
la relazione relationship
il rene kidney (body part)
il repellente per gli insetti insect
  repellent
il residente UE EU resident
respirare v breathe
il ricambio part (for car)
il riciclaggio n recycling
la ricetta prescription
ricevere v receive
la ricevuta receipt
il riciclaggio n recycling
riempire v fill
rifiutare v decline (credit card)
ringraziare v thank
riparare v fix, mend, repair
ripetere v repeat
ripido steep
il responsabile manager
il riscaldamento heating
riscaldare v warm (something)
la riserva naturale nature preserve
i risparmi savings (account)
il ristorante restaurant
ritardare v delay
ritirare v withdraw

il ritiro bagagli baggage claim
la riunione meeting
la rivista magazine
romantico romantic
rompere v break
rosa pink
rosso red
rotto broken
la roulotte trailer
le rovine ruins
rubare v rob, steal
rubato stolen
il rugby rugby
il rullino film (camera)
il ruscello stream

S

il sacchetto per i rifiuti garbage
[rubbish BE] bag
il sacco a pelo sleeping bag
la sala room; **~ congressi**
convention hall; **~ d'attesa**
waiting room; **~ da concerti**
concert hall; **~ da pranzo** dining
room; **~ giochi** arcade;
~ riunioni meeting room
il salone di bellezza nail salon
la salute health
Salute! Cheers!
salvare v save (computer)
salve hello

la salvietta per neonati baby
wipe
i sandali sandals
il sangue blood
sanguinare v bleed
il santuario shrine
il sapone soap
la sauna sauna
la sbornia hangover
le scale stairs; **~**
mobili escalators
lo scanner scanner
le scarpe shoes;
~ da neve snowshoes;
~ basse flat shoes; **~ col tacco**
alto high-heeled shoes;
~ da ginnastica sneakers
gli scarponi da montagna hiking
boots
la scatola box
lo scatolame canned good
scendere v get off (a train, bus,
subway)
la scheda card; **~ memoria**
memory card; **~ telefonica**
phone card
lo schermo display
la schiena back (body part)
lo sci n ski; **~ d'acqua** water skis
sciare v ski
la sciarpa scarf

la scienza science

scippare v mug

la scogliera cliff

la scolapasta colander

scollegare v disconnect (computer)

lo scollo a V V-neck

scommettere v place a bet

scomparso missing

lo sconto discount

lo scontrino bagagli luggage [baggage BE] ticket

lo scooter moped

la scopa broom

la scottatura sunburn

scrivere v spell, write

la scuola school

scuro dark

scusare v excuse

scusi sorry (apology)

sedersi v sit

la sedia chair; **~ a rotelle** wheelchair; **~ a sdraio** deck chair

il sedile per bambino child's seat

il seggiolino per auto car seat

il seggiolone highchair

la seggiovia chair lift

il self-service self-service

il semaforo traffic light

il seminario seminar

il senso unico one-way street

il sentiero path, trail

senza without; **~ grassi** fat free; **~ piombo** unleaded (gas)

separato separated (marriage)

la sera evening

serio serious

la serratura n lock

i servizi di pulizia domestica housekeeping services

il servizio service (in a restaurant); **~ completo** full-service; **~ di lavanderia** laundry service; **~ in camera** room service; **~ Internet** internet service; **~ Internet wireless** wireless internet service; **~ sveglia** wake-up call

la seta silk

la settimana week

settimanalmente weekly

lo shampoo shampoo

lo shopping shopping

sì yes

la sicurezza security

sicuro safe (protected)

la sigaretta cigarette

il sigaro cigar

il simbolo symbol (keyboard)

la sinagoga synagogue

single single (marriage)

lo ski lift drag lift, ski lift

lo slip briefs (clothing)

lo smalto enamel (jewelry)
lo snack bar snack bar
lo snowboard snowboard
il sole sun
soleggiato sunny
solo alone, only; **~ andata** one-way (ticket)
la soluzione per lenti a contatto contact lens solution
la sonnolenza drowsiness
sopra over
sordo deaf
la sorella sister
il sottotitolo subtitle
il souvenir souvenir
la spalla shoulder
la spatola spatula
la spazzatura trash [rubbish BE]
la spazzola hairbrush
lo specialista specialist (doctor)
la specialità special (food)
spedire v mail
spegnere v turn off (lights)
lo spettacolo n play (theater); **~ di danza** ballet
la spiaggia beach
la spilla brooch
la spina dorsale spine (body part)
spingere v push (door sign)
lo spogliatoio fitting room

sporco dirty
lo sport sport
sposare v marry
sposato married
la spuntatina trim (hair)
la squadra team
squisito delicious
lo stadio stadium
lo stagno pond
stampare v print
la stampa n print; **~ digitale** digital print; **~ singola** single print
stanco tired
stanotte tonight
la stanza room
stare v stay
gli Stati Uniti United States (U.S.)
la station wagon station wagon [estate car BE]
la statua statue
la stazione station; **~ degli autobus** bus station; **~ dei bus** bus station; **~ ferroviaria** train station [railway station BE]; **~ della metropolitana** subway station [underground station BE]; **~ di servizio** gas station [petrol station BE]; **~ termale** spa
la stecca di sigarette carton of cigarettes

le sterline pounds (British sterling)
stesso same
stirare v iron, press (clothing)
gli stivali boots
lo stomaco stomach; **~ in disordine** upset stomach
stordito dizzy
la storta sprain
strano strange
straordinario amazing
lo studente student
studiare v study
stuprare v rape
lo stupro n rape
lo sturalavandini plunger
sud south
la super super (fuel)
superiore upper
il supermercato supermarket
la supervisione supervision
svegliare, svegliarsi v wake
sviluppare v develop (film)
svuotare v empty

T

il tabaccaio tobacconist
la taglia size; **~ forte** plus size
tagliare v cut (hair)
il taglio n cut (injury), haircut
il tampone tampon
tardi late (time)

la tariffa fee
la tasca pocket
la tassa duty (tax)
il tasso di cambio exchange rate
la tavola da surf surfboard
il tavolo table
il taxi taxi
la tazza cup; **~ di misurazione** measuring cup
il teatro theater; **~ dell'opera** opera house
telefonare v phone
la telefonata phone call
il telefonino cell [mobile BE] phone
il telefono n phone; **~ telephone**; **~ cordless** wireless phone; **~ pubblico** pay phone
il telone impermeabile groundcloth [groundsheet BE]
il tempio temple (religious)
il tempo time, weather
la tenda tent
il tennis tennis
la terapia ad ossigeno oxygen treatment
le terme hot spring
il terminal terminal (airport)
la terracotta terracotta
terribile terrible
la tessera card; **~ associativa**

membership card;
~ **dell'assicurazione** insurance
card; ~ **internazionale dello**
studente international student
card

la testa head (body part)

il testo *n* text (message)

tirare *v* pull (door sign)

la toilette restroom [toilet BE]

la torcia elettrica flashlight

la torre tower

la tosse *n* cough

tossire *v* cough

il totale total (amount)

il tovagliolo napkin

tradizionale traditional

tradurre *v* translate

il traghetto ferry

tranquillo quiet

trasferire *v* transfer (money)

il travellers cheque travelers check
[travelers cheque BE]

il treno train; ~ **espresso** express
train

triste sad

troppo too

tuffarsi *v* dive

il turista tourist

la TV TV

U

l'uccello bird

l'ufficio office; ~ **di**
cambio currency
exchange office; ~
informazioni information desk;
~ **informazioni turistiche**
tourist information office; ~
oggetti smarriti lost and
found; ~ **postale** post office; ~
prenotazioni reservation desk

ultimo last

una volta once

l'unghia fingernail, toenail

unire *v* join

l'università university

uno one

l'uomo man

urgente urgent

usa e getta disposable

usare *v* use

uscire *v* exit

l'uscita gate (airport), exit;
~ **d'emergenza** emergency exit

l'utensile utensil

V

la vacanza vacation [holiday BE]

la vaccinazione vaccination

la vagina vagina

il vagone letto sleeper [sleeping

BE] car
valido valid
la valigia suitcase
la valle valley
il valore value
la valuta currency
il vaso jar
vecchio old
vedere v see
vedovo widowed
vegetariano vegetarian
il veleno poison
veloce fast
vendere v sell
venire v come
il ventaglio fan (souvenir)
il ventilatore fan (appliance)
il verbale di polizia police report
verde green
vero real
la vescica bladder
il vestito dress (piece of clothing)
la vetrina window case
la vetrinetta display case
il vetro glass (material)
la vetta peak (of a mountain)
il viaggio trip

vicino close, near, nearby, next to
i vigili del fuoco fire department
il vigneto vineyard
il villaggio village
viola purple
la visita turistica sightseeing
visitare v visit
il viso face
il visto visa
la vita life
la vitamina vitamin
vivere v live
il volo flight; ~ **internazionale**
  international flight; ~ **nazionale**
  domestic flight
vomitare v vomit

W

il WC da campeggio chemical
  toilet
il windsurf windsurfer

Z

lo zaino backpack
la zona area; ~ **commerciale**
  shopping area; ~ **picnic** picnic
  area
lo zoo zoo

Berlitz®

speaking your language

phrase book & dictionary
phrase book & CD

Available in: Arabic, Brazilian Portuguese*, Burmese*, Cantonese
Chinese, Croatian, Czech*, Danish*, Dutch, English, Filipino, Finnish*, French,
German, Greek, Hebrew*, Hindi*, Hungarian*, Indonesian, Italian, Japanese,
Korean, Latin American Spanish, Malay, Mandarin Chinese, Mexican Spanish,
Norwegian, Polish, Portuguese, Romanian*, Russian, Spanish, Swedish, Thai,
Turkish, Vietnamese
*Book only

www.berlitzpublishing.com